Trainer's
Diversity
Source Book

Ask for the accompanying software at
the circulation desk in this Library

HR Source Book Series

Trainer's Diversity
Source Book

50 Ready-to-Use Activities
from Icebreakers through Wrap Ups

Jonamay Lambert and Selma Myers

Society for Human Resource Management
Alexandria, Virginia
USA
www.shrm.org

ASTD
Alexandria, Virginia
USA
www.astd.org

This publication is designed to provide accurate and authoritative information regarding the subject matter covered. It is sold with the understanding that neither the publishers nor the authors are engaged in rendering legal or other professional service. If legal advice or other expert assistance is required, the services of a competent, licensed professional should be sought. The federal and state laws discussed in this book are subject to frequent revision and interpretation by amendments or judicial revisions that may significantly affect employer or employee rights and obligations. Readers are encouraged to seek legal counsel regarding specific policies and practices in their organizations.

This book is co-published by the Society for Human Resource Management (SHRM®) and the American Society for Training and Development (ASTD). The interpretations, conclusions, and recommendations in this book are those of the authors and do not necessarily represent those of SHRM or ASTD.

The Society for Human Resource Management (SHRM) is the world's largest association devoted to human resource management. Representing more than 190,000 individual members, the Society serves the needs of HR professionals by providing the most essential and comprehensive set of resources available. As an influential voice, SHRM is committed to advancing the human resource profession to ensure that HR is an essential and effective partner in developing and executing organizational strategy. Visit SHRM Online at **www.shrm.org**.

ASTD is a leading association of workplace learning and performance professionals, forming a world-class community of practice. ASTD's 70,000 members and associates come from more than 100 countries and thousands of organizations—multinational corporations, medium-sized and small businesses, government, academia, consulting firms, and product and service suppliers. ASTD marks its beginning in 1944 when the organization held its first annual conference. In recent years, ASTD has widened the industry's focus to connect learning and performance to measurable results, and is a sought-after voice on critical public policy issues. For more information, visit **www.astd.org** or call 800.628.2783 (International 703.683.8100).

Library of Congress Cataloging-in-Publication Data

Lambert, Jonamay.
    Trainer's diversity source book : 50 ready-to-use activities, from icebreakers through wrap ups / Jonamay Lambert and Selma Myers.— 1st ed.
        p. cm. — (HR source book series)
    ISBN 1-58644-063-2
    1. Diversity in the workplace. 2. Employees—Training of. I. Myers, Selma. II. Title. III. Series.

HF5549.5.M5L358 2004
658.3'008—dc22

                                2004020100

Printed in the United States of America.
10 9 8 7 6 5 4 3 2 1

Contents

Acknowledgments

We would like to acknowledge several wonderful people who have helped make this book possible. They gave us encouragement during the writing of the book and were there for us in various ways. Listening, sharing ideas and experiences, and supporting us through the production trials and tribulations resulted in what we hope and believe will be a great resource.

First, we want to acknowledge Gretchen Neve, Senior Associate with Lambert & Associates for her support and contributions to the book. Not only was Gretchen our project manager, she participated in the actual writing and devoted endless hours to editing.

Second, we would also like to extend a special thank you to Gloria Cotton, Instructional Designer, and Senior Associate with Lambert & Associates for the upgrades on many of the activities.

Also, we feel fortunate to have such a positive team and want to especially thank the following people: From Lambert & Associates, Inc: Lorren Cotton, Client Solutions Coordinator; Scott Hoesman, Vice President; Lisa Childs Johnson, Senior Associate; Brian Sorge, V.P. Client Solutions; and Joseph Wheeler, Independent Consultant. And Lucy Schaeffer, Owner, L&S Secretarial.

Thanks also go to the following substantive reviewers whose time, effort, and excellent advice resulted in a better book: Lee Gardenswartz and Anita Rowe of Gardenswartz & Rowe; Gregory M. Davis, Esq., Seyfarth Shaw LLP; and Maxine Kamin, TOUCH Consulting, Inc.

Finally, we would like to thank Laura Lawson for her keen interest, support, encouragement and flexibility.

Chapter 1
Overview

We know what we are, but know not what we may be.
WILLIAM SHAKESPEARE

Globalization and accelerated change, along with increasingly multicultural organizations and teams are today's workplace realities. People of all occupations face increasing demands from their organizations. In this climate, everyone—executives, managers, supervisors, administrators, and employees from all functions—benefits from learning about diversity and developing the competencies that help people get work done more efficiently and effectively.

The main theme of this book is that we can explore ideas and learn about diversity in brief, interesting, and captivating ways. Learning about diversity is valuable in all kinds of organizations from education and government to businesses and not-for-profits. In fact, this learning is essential to building and developing an inclusive organization.

"Inclusive" describes organizations that attract, develop, retain and promote talented people. Creating a climate that values diversity means that talented people from differing backgrounds and with varying experience will feel included. Inclusive organizations are competitive and successful in today's business environment. It turns out that creating an environment where all employees and customers are valued and appreciated is good for business.

Defining Diversity
In this book, when we refer to "diversity," we mean "the collection of similarities and differences that we carry with us at all times based on characteristics we were born with, experiences we have had, and choices we have made." In this context, everyone is diverse.

Getting to know people is how we discover what makes them unique as individuals. Recognizing that uniqueness—or their diversity—helps us draw on everyone's talent, strengths, and enthusiasm to produce the best possible outcome on a project or a task. A distinguishing characteristic of high-achieving teams is that they engage people's passion. Each person on the team knows that she or he is essential to success. No one feels disposable because no one is disposable. All talent is developed and tapped.

Behaviors and beliefs, once thought to be insignificant in business, have become major considerations. A common assumption is that people and businesses are the same all over. This really means that we think that people and businesses all over are "just like us." In reality, people have different thought patterns, work ethics, business philosophies, beliefs, personal histories, cultural traditions, and values that actively shape behavior and priorities at home and in the workplace.

Who Is This Book For?

This book provides trainers with brief and interesting activities that increase workshop participants' awareness of diversity in nonthreatening ways and bring home positive points about diversity issues. We hope it will be useful to people who have been in diversity work for a long time as well as to people who are new to the field. As the title suggests, we have included activities that can be used at various points during training when setting up, warming up, or wrapping up a session. Some activities also are energizers that can be used in the middle of the day.

While these activities are useful in a session focusing on diversity, they can be useful in other kinds of training, including sessions focusing on management development, leadership development, and supervisory skills. They are equally appropriate for new employee orientations, communication skills training, and conflict resolution programs.

What Are Diversity Activities?

These diversity activities are learning activities that add interest and can be used in a number of ways. Some are icebreakers—brief activities designed to get people talking to each other. Still others introduce a specific topic or prompt further examination of a topic in a relatively brief yet interesting way. Expanded versions of some of our basic activities create opportunities for more in-depth conversations. Other components that can be included in a session about diversity might include simulations, special topic videos, or diversity-related games.

The awareness and skills brought out by the activities in this book can be put to use at any stage of diversity awareness and skills, starting with the early exploration of the topic, continuing with improved information and growth, and finally developing some feeling of confidence and an interest in taking action.

All of the activities in this book are designed to facilitate dialogues and encourage open-minded listening. They offer opportunities for self-reflection, honest talk, and even a little humor. The goals are for participants to leave the room with new insights into themselves and others, and to help them work with others more effectively when they return to their daily work.

Legal Issues

While we have not experienced any legal issues related to diversity training, that's not to say others haven't. Whether you are an outside consultant or in-house trainer, prior to conducting your training it is a good idea to ask for direction and probe for any sensitivities that may exist related to this topic. We suggest that outside consultants have a discussion with their clients and in-house trainers at least consider their own knowledge of their companies about the following issues:

- Potential or recent complaints or legal actions.

- Union sensitivities.

- Language and terminology to avoid.

- Similar training that has occurred in the past.

- Similar or related training.

Here are a few suggestions to keep in mind as you design and deliver your diversity training.

- Make sure when introducing language or policies that the organization is REALLY committed to them. Read and understand the diversity policies or statements.

- There may be union issues that impact employee attendance, particularly if the training is not during their normal work schedules.

- Link diversity skills to job requirements and behavioral expectations.

- Some organizations may ask their legal department or outside counsel to review the training program. Be aware that legal departments tend to:
  - Check for consistency.
  - Watch for tone.
  - Avoid making commitment to changes in policies and practices. For example, trainers should not imply that changes will necessarily result from discussions.
  - Ensure that no "new" terminology is being introduced to the company's lexicon, presumably because these new terms have not been tested and there is no precedent supporting their usage. For example, the phrase "world views" or "nationality" may not have been used in the company before and may be problematic to the legal department.

- If situations that you are unsure about how to handle come up in the workshop, it is best to refer the participant to appropriate internal resources, such as to the human resources department.

- Pilot the diversity training first to human resource and diversity specialists.

- Create and obtain consensus on "learning guidelines" or "ground rules" that create an environment where participants feel safe discussing workplace experiences and can practice appropriate interpersonal skills and expected behaviors. Reach an agreement on confidentiality and on what is permissible to discuss in class (and what is not).

■ If managers and line supervisors attend training with employees who report directly to them, they should be advised on any organizational policies regarding disclosure of work-related diversity issues.

■ After training is conducted, remove all flipchart papers and other materials that were not handed out to all participants. These materials could be misconstrued.

■ Inform participants where they can go to discuss concerns or provide feedback related to the diversity training program.

■ Provide written workshop evaluations to assess content, facilitator performance and methodology.

Know Your Audience

It is important to know who will be in your audience so that you select the appropriate activities. For example, if you have participants with physical disabilities you will want to ensure that they can fully participate or will want to redesign the activity to meet their needs. For example, to accommodate a person in a wheelchair, an activity that requires people to physically move through an obstacle course may require having larger obstacles and a change in physical layout. For people with visual impairments, you may need to enlarge print on handouts and overheads. It may be necessary to have an interpreter for those who are deaf or hearing impaired.

If you have people in your audience who don't speak English, you may need a translator.

Bottom line, prior to any design or delivery of training it is critical for you to know who will be attending and to design and deliver training that includes all participants.

Selecting and Using Activities in this Book

It is important to select and facilitate activities with good judgment and care. Because participants and groups have different levels and kinds of experiences with these diversity topics, each group may respond in different ways.

In Chapter 2 we offer basic facilitation tips to overcome some of the challenges and pitfalls encountered in diversity training. Case studies of real-life situations are used to describe situations that could have derailed a workshop. These are followed by important facilitation points that saved the day. The chapter also contains other useful suggestions that you can use to make your facilitation fun, practical, and effective.

This book offers you many useful tips and materials. Ultimately, however, the most important ingredient in the mix is you. You know best what you want to achieve, and it is up to you to use or adapt the materials to achieve the desired outcome.

Activities may include the elements below. If an activity uses handouts, prepared flipchart pages, or other prepared materials, models for these items follow the activity.

- Time required.

- Objectives.

- Equipment.

- Materials.

- Handouts.

- Procedures.

- Discussion questions.

- Key points.

- Trainer's notes.

Some activities offer expanded versions that may include additional procedures or debriefing questions.

The Activity Matrix that follows alphabetically lists each matrix activity, its primary topic as well as the activities that offer an expanded version.

Activity Matrix

Activity Name	Getting to Know Each Other	Setting the Climate	Personal Awareness	Values	Assumptions and Stereotypes	Communication	Diversity Issues	Conflict Resolution	Team Building	Energizers	Wrapping Up	Expanded Version
Checking Assumptions Scenario					X							X
Choices			X									X
Circle Game		X										X
Close Encounters of the First Kind			X									
Connections	X											X
Cultural Introductions			X									X
Decades on Parade			X									X
Diversity Groundhog							X					X
Do You See What I See?					X							X
Double or Nothing								X				X
Doves or Hawks— Individual Conflict Styles								X				X
Even Exchange					X							
Finding Commonalities		X										X
Getting Out of the Fishbowl							X					X
History Channel	X											
How Do You Say "Hello"?										X		X
How Far to Push?								X				X
I Belong	X											X
I Can't See for Looking						X						X
I See, You See... Changing Lenses					X							X
If I Were in Your Shoes							X					X
Kindergarten Incident								X				X
Knee-jerk Response			X									X
Million-Dollar Question				X								X
Name Tags R Us	X											X
Nonverbal Introduction						X						X
One Potato, Two Potato					X							
Optimizing Team Diversity									X			X
Pulse Check										X		X

Activity Matrix Continued

Activity Name	Getting to Know Each Other	Setting the Climate	Personal Awareness	Values	Assumptions and Stereotypes	Communication	Diversity Issues	Conflict Resolution	Team Building	Energizers	Wrapping Up	Expanded Version
Setting New Directions											X	X
Sharing Cultural Stories, Legends, Tales			X									X
Statistics at a Glance	X											X
Ticket to Talk						X						
Time Waits for No One											X	
Trading Value Cards				X								X
Treasure Hunt		X										X
Understanding Commitment									X			X
Value Line				X								X
Values, Values, Values				X								X
Vision of Diversity and Inclusion												X
What about Positive Stereotypes?					X							X
What Does it Mean to You?					X							X
What's in a Name?	X											X
What's on Your Mind?						X						X
When You C.A.R.E. Enough		X										X
Why Diversity and Inclusion?		X										X
Win a Few, Lose A Few!							X					
Words of Wisdom											X	X
ZAP Model					X							X

The book organizes the activities as follows.

Chapter 3, Getting to Know Each Other, presents activities that begin building relationships among participants in ways related to diversity and inclusion.

Chapter 4, Setting the Climate, presents activities that create the session's climate for learning and establish ways in which valuing diversity and building inclusiveness benefits organizations, employees, and customers.

Chapter 5, Personal Awareness, presents activities that increase each participant's awareness of his or her own cultural heritage(s) and uniqueness.

Chapter 6, Values, presents activities that increase participants' awareness of personal and cultural values and how they influence behavior.

Chapter 7, Assumptions and Stereotypes, presents activities that increase awareness about perception, assumptions, and stereotypes that impact us consciously and unconsciously and explore what we can do about it.

Chapter 8, Communication, presents activities that explore aspects of communication to help build relationships and increase understanding when faced with diversity.

Chapter 9, Diversity Issues, presents activities that explore specific topics of diversity and ways of addressing them effectively.

Chapter 10, Conflict Resolution, presents activities that increase awareness of habitual ways of dealing with conflict and identify alternatives strategies that work more effectively.

Chapter 11, Team Building, presents activities that explore ways of building teams that optimize their diversity and enhance inclusiveness.

Chapter 12, Energizers, presents activities that can be used at any time to quickly energize a group.

Chapter 13, Wrapping Up, presents activities for action planning and ending a session.

Chapter 14, Resources, includes:

- A list of Web sites we have found to be helpful in keeping current with new information, books, and other diversity-related products;

- Quotable quotes and suggestions for how to use them as a diversity activity;

- Templates for diversity-related communications;

- Creative ways of selecting volunteers; and

- Information about the contents of the accompanying CD-ROM.

Many sources are available to help you learn about diversity and inclusion, among them great books and magazines and an ever-growing list of videos. The resources listed in chapter 14 include Web sites we have found helpful in keeping current on trends and research.

This book comes with a CD-ROM, with the following materials in PDF and RTF formats for easy use and customization:

- The Activity Matrix from this chapter;

- All activities and their accompanying materials;

- Quotable quotes and suggestions for how to use them;

- A list of helpful Web sites;

- Templates for communication; and

- Creative ways to select "volunteers."

We hope that including these materials on the CD-ROM will make it easy for facilitators to customize our activities for their organizations and workshops.

Benefits of Diversity Training

There are many ways to learn about diversity and inclusion. There are great books, magazines, Web sites, and an ever-growing list of videos.

While intellectual knowledge is important, it doesn't necessarily change behavior. If we want to apply intellectual knowledge to change behavior and decisions, learning about diversity also must engage the heart. And the way to engage the heart is to create opportunities for interaction and dialogue among people. Activities that do this distinguish workshop learning from book learning. As participants more fully understand their own uniqueness and diversity along with the uniqueness and diversity of others, they discover how incorrect assumptions and unconscious stereotypes have been shaping their decisions and behavior. They also learn about how decisions and behavior affect others in ways they had not even imagined. The road to freedom, conscious choice, and unleashing the power of human potential lies in knowledge and self-awareness. We hope that these activities contribute to that effort.

Chapter 2
Tips and Tricks of Facilitating

Greetings! I am pleased to see that we are different.
May we together become greater than the sum of both of us.

MR. SPOCK (ON THE TELEVISION SERIES *STAR TREK*)

Our belief is that great facilitators are not necessarily born as great facilitators. There is a little mixing of art and science to facilitation. In this chapter, we share some common facilitator challenges and pitfalls, along with tips for surmounting them.

First, we provide some basic content and suggestions. Next, we share case studies of real-life situations that could have derailed a workshop. Last we present important facilitation points that saved the day. The chapter also contains other useful suggestions that you can use to make your facilitation fun, practical, and effective.

Before we begin, it's important to define what your role as a facilitator actually means. This book offers you many useful tips and materials. Ultimately, however, the most important ingredient in the mix is you. You know best what you want to achieve, and it is up to you to use or adapt the materials to achieve the desired outcome.

Diversity is a subject that may require both training and facilitation. It is important to understand how the roles of trainer and facilitator differ. If you are giving information about or demonstrating a specific skill, you probably are acting as a trainer. The teaching process may be very interactive, but the content is specific and the primary goal is to convey your knowledge and skill to the learner. By contrast, facilitation is a teaching method designed to stimulate questions that lead to self-discovery. As a facilitator, you may present information, set up an activity, and ask questions, but at a critical point you step back to let the learners find their own way to the desired knowledge and insights.

When the goal is raising awareness about diversity, facilitation is the preferred delivery approach. The activities used leverage participants' experiences, knowledge, skills, attitudes, and so forth. Typically, the facilitator is engaged in managing a process rather than developing and focusing on content.

Some common facilitator challenges and pitfalls are:

■ Creating a welcoming environment;

■ Handling discussions of values and beliefs sensitively and effectively;

■ Managing our own "stuff" (judgments, stereotypes, biases, and blind spots); and

■ Dealing with difficult participants.

Creating a Welcoming Environment

Getting off to the right start establishes a positive learning atmosphere. Your actions, words, and body language send powerful messages. Remember, setting the tone up front will greatly influence the outcome. The environment you want to create will:

■ Encourage open and full participation;

■ Allow participants to share personal attitudes and opinions; and

■ Create an environment that is open, safe, thought-provoking, and fun.

There are many things you can do to promote a positive learning environment. For example, you can:

■ Involve participants from the start. Use a quick icebreaker before the workshop even begins. An example of a suitable icebreaker is "Connections" in Chapter 3.

■ Speak to the participants and about the participants. Use "you" language rather than "I" language. Try, "You are going to learn so much from each other that, when you leave the workshop, you will find that you have new resources you can tap in to."

■ Define your role. You are the facilitator, not the expert. Remember that the workshop is about the participants—not you. See "What's In A Name" in Chapter 3 for a sample introduction you might use or adapt.

■ Establish learning guidelines. Engage the participants in setting rules for the way they want to work together. We've provided some examples in "When You C.A.R.E. in Chapter 3. Encourage both positive and negative feedback. Make it OK for people to be honest about their feelings. Remember that some participants may not be attending the workshop by choice.

■ Use sights, sounds and smells. Play some music before the workshop starts and during breaks. In some contexts, we've even used candles. Plan interesting ways to reconvene the full group from small-group discussion or activities, such as using chimes, whistles, bells, etc.

■ Be creative with your flipcharts. Use colors, designs, and other techniques to liven them up rather than just writing them in the same old black or brown markers.

■ Divide the participants into groups in interesting ways such as counting off, using playing cards, or passing out colored dots at the beginning.

■ Show interest in others. Learn about your participants. Socialize during breaks or over lunch. Share some personal information about yourself.

Have fun yourself! The topic of diversity can be intimidating for many people. There may be topics that bring up strong emotions for some participants, as well as serious conversations and differences of opinion, but the session can still be fun.

The cases below are based on actual experiences and have been provided by a number of Lambert facilitators.

At one real workshop, the facilitator's barely-on-time arrival clouded the entire session. As you read this case study, think about how you might have handled the situation.

Case Study: Timing is Everything

When I began working as a facilitator, I was told to make sure that I got to the training site early enough to get my flipcharts prepared, set out participant materials, and handle last-minute logistics. Once all that was done, I would be ready to welcome participants.

I knew that "welcoming participants" was the polite thing to do, but I didn't realize how important it is in setting the tone until I attended a training session where the facilitator got there "just in time." Although he was ready to go at the session's start time, I'm not sure we were. It took a while for us to warm up to him and the program.

In contrast, at a training session a few months later, the facilitator had handled all the logistics and welcomed us to the session the way a host would welcome you to his home. As a result, before that training had even started, people began talking and even welcoming other people as they came in the door. The tone set by that facilitator created an environment that encouraged openness and dialogue. I have never forgotten the effect of the tone he set.

Case Resolution

It is easy to overlook the importance of welcoming people to a session. But for a session devoted to diversity—where the overall aim is to focus on increasing inclusiveness and learning about working effectively together—providing a warm welcome may be more important than ever. Be ready to introduce yourself as participants arrive, even before the session starts. Shaking hands with participants and being available for conversation helps to create a friendly environment. Of course, beware of talking more with the people who keep you in your "comfort zone": Make sure to welcome everyone. Breaks and lunch are also great times to touch base with people and follow up on discussions from the session.

Effectively Handling Discussions about Values and Beliefs

Discussion of values and beliefs is a critical part of understanding differences. Beliefs and values drive behavior: Every decision we make is influenced consciously or unconsciously by our values, beliefs, and attitudes. According to Dr. Albert Mehrabian, 90 percent of our values are formed by the time we are 10 years old.

Discussing values can be controversial and emotional. In particular, the following topics can be emotional and controversial:

Religion	Family
Money	Rules or authority
Politics	Work
War and peace	Education

Often, such topics are laden with beliefs and attitudes about what is "good," "bad," "right," or "wrong." As a facilitator, being able to identify and understand your personal values is a prerequisite to engaging others in dialogue on such topics.

Remember that when facilitating value related discussions, the goal is not necessarily to reach consensus. Rather, it is to help participants see beyond their personal outlooks and examine how their values may play out for others.

In one workshop, a participant's reaction to a topic challenged the facilitator. As you read this case study, think how you might have handled the situation.

Case Study: Moral Objection

I was engaged in a large-group discussion activity that had participants define diversity. When one participant stated that sexual orientation should be included in the definition, there was a mixed reaction from the group.

Some group members agreed, others remained silent, and then one participant insisted that sexual orientation shouldn't even be a part of a workplace discussion. Several group members challenged him and he became defensive. He went so far as to say, "I would be ashamed if my younger son learns that our company would even consider recognizing 'those' people. Homosexuality is against God's commandments, and if we start allowing that then the next thing that would happen is that it would be OK for people to have sex with animals." There was dead silence in the room and all eyes were on me.

Case Resolution

Review learning behavioral guidelines that have been established as a group. Remind participants that it is OK to disagree and restate the importance of using sensitivity and respect when doing so. Do not get into a debate. Use the discussion as a way to demonstrate how different beliefs are learned and how they affect the decisions we make. Challenge participants to identify where the values they hold have originated. More often than not, our values have been taught to us by parents, churches, schools, the news media, and peers. Often people do not question the values they hold or examine the contradictions between a value they may hold and the behavior that supports that value. Give—and ask for—examples, such as:

- People who believe in freedom of speech yet deny it to people with different opinions from their own; and

- People who regularly go to religious services and profess to "love their neighbors" but otherwise either don't talk to neighbors or gossip about them.

Encourage participants to think about alternative ways of thinking and acting that encourage sharing, honesty, and respect. Model effective listening and observation skills—both verbal as well as nonverbal. Seek to understand, and do not impose your values on others. Be aware of whether you are listening for participants to tell you what you want to hear.

Remind participants that the workshop is designed to help them recognize, understand and challenge their values—not to change them. Only they can do that.

- Remember that while values may not change, our workplace behaviors can.

- Point out that the more choices we have the more complex our decisions about values may be.

Managing Our Own "Stuff"

Before doing this type of facilitation, it is critical that we have done our own work on diversity issues. We all make judgments. All of us—even facilitators—have our own stereotypes, biases, and blind spots. We're all human. We all need to continue learning and growing. Here are a few suggestions to further your growth as a diversity facilitator:

- Attend professional conferences.

- Share your experiences with other colleagues.

- Ask for suggestions from others in the field.

- Read and stay current on the topics related to diversity.

- Have a respected colleague observe you in action and ask for feedback.

- Keep an open mind.

- Be willing to admit when you don't understand an issue.

- Be honest with yourself about your own "hot buttons."

In a few workshops, facilitators have found their own "stuff" a challenge. As you read each case study, think about how you might have handled the situation.

Case Study: Me, Too!

I'm a forty-ish white woman—this data about me becomes relevant later in my story. It was my first time facilitating a new half-day diversity workshop. Despite years of experience, each time I work with a new program, I get nervous. It takes me about four times facilitating a new program before I understand the rhythm and flow of the curriculum.

In addition, two observers were in the room so they could give me feedback. It was important that the session go well, as I wanted to make a good impression. Talk about pressure!

One-third of the way through, all was going along well enough. Then a white male participant said in response to a question that I had asked, "Yeah, if I'm going through an alley and I see a black guy, I keep my eye on him and hurry up to get out of there."

At that moment, half of my brain froze. I was on the hot seat as facilitator. How was I going to respond? I thought, "I can't believe that he just said this. How are the two African American people in the room doing? I felt like my job as the facilitator was to make sure they were OK and that I didn't think what was said was OK. I didn't want anyone to think that I might be racist—or a wimp facilitator!" I also didn't want my response to make participant who made the comment defensive and resistant.

Case Resolution

Thank participants for sharing and for being honest. Respond directly and immediately to comments—not later and indirectly. Acknowledge that everyone has biases and have been consciously or unconsciously impacted by racism. It is sometimes helpful to share a personal experience. Here is an example this facilitator shared: A white diversity colleague got a streak of insight when he realized that when he passed black men on the street, he habitually averted his gaze or even crossed the street. That insight was fairly disturbing and humbling—he had discovered a potent way in which a stereotype had been shaping his behavior without his conscious knowledge.

One day, a young black man was walking directly toward him. His internal alarm bells went off. He was ready to cross the street when he remembered his insight and decided to resist the impulse to flee. This did not mean that he felt safe. All his impulses said, "Cross this street now!" Yet he chose to not act on them.

The young man came up and asked him for directions because he was lost. He was relieved (and embarrassed at his relief). He walked the young man to his destination, realizing that his help had really made a difference.

At another workshop, the facilitator's ability to work with her own "stuff" made a positive difference. As you read this case, think how you might have handled the situation.

Case Study: Difference of Opinion

In a session after we had established ground rules that included respectful communication, a male participant stated, respectfully, that he considered diversity to be a code for "minorities exercising the power of their will over the majority."

A lesbian in the session responded by sharing how the company's positive stance toward gay and lesbian employees created an environment that invited her loyalty and made her more productive. She shared that she had created a decal of the rainbow colors to wear on her identification badge so others would know she is lesbian.

The male participant's response was that it offended him to have her announce her sexual orientation via the decal. The environment was very tense, but the tone, while disagreeable, was never disrespectful.

Case Resolution

Thank participants for being willing to share their opinions in a respectful way.

Check in with both participants to make sure they are OK and that they felt they had been heard.

As a facilitator, be mindful not to let your own discomfort with disagreements lead you to shut down a conversation too soon. Remember that as long as a discussion takes place within the guidelines of respect, all positions are important to be viewed—not just those you agree with.

Repeating the positions without taking sides is a key to diminishing resistance. Acknowledge the level of the tension in the room keeps participants in the present moment.

In another workshop, the facilitator came face-to-face with certain assumptions. As you read this case, think how you might have handled the situation.

Case Study: Challenging Assumptions

The opening of a program included an exercise to have participants express how they felt about being in a diversity training session. In previous sessions, the participants who expressed the most discomfort had tended to be white men, with others demonstrating various higher levels of comfort.

In one session, however, the participant with the greatest negative reaction was a woman who was also the only person of color in the room. I immediately began assessing why she would be negative about her company supporting diversity and speculated about a number of reasons about why she would deny her experience as a woman of color.

Later in the day, we had the opportunity to talk, and she shared that the reason she initially had negative thoughts was that she questioned whether a one-day training program would make any difference. She had seen other diversity programs at this company that promised to make a difference, but she felt that each had been disappointing. She expected this to be another one. She was deeply committed to diversity, but not to the training. As the day progressed, she became very engaged, shared her own personal experience, and became a supporter of the process.

Case Resolution

Do not presume that people who are not in the majority support the diversity program. More importantly, do not presume to know why people respond the way they do. Their motives may be outside our scope of experience and understanding. In diversity training it becomes particularly important for the facilitator to watch and honor others' experiences, and when appropriate, to ask questions about why people take the positions that they do.

Dealing with Difficult Participants

Challenging participants present themselves in a variety of situations and reveal themselves by displaying a variety of behaviors. Remember, people come with all types of personalities. Regardless of the welcoming environment you have established and your best facilitation skills, there will always be "difficult" participants. The key to managing these situations is to be able to understand what is causing them to begin with.

Here are a few of the personality-related problems that typically occur in workshops when participants have:

- Dominating personalities;
- Antagonistic personalities; and
- Argumentative personalities.

Dominating Personalities

The typical behaviors you might experience from a participant with a dominating personality are always having something to say or wanting to monopolize the discussion.

What can you do?

Identify these participants quickly and determine the best approach that will not shut them down but will limit the amount of time they speak. One way of doing this is to tactfully interrupt by saying something like, "Great point, let's hear from others." You can also call on others first. If necessary, have a private conversation with the person and express your appreciation for the person's contributions but ask for his or her assistance in making it possible for others to contribute as well.

Antagonistic Personalities

Usually antagonistic participants didn't want to attend the program to start with and feel that they have nothing to gain from it. One way to engage participants like this is to discuss the WIIFM (What's In It For Me?) of the program. Another possibility is to directly ask the individual to participate and to remain nonjudgmental until the workshop is over. Try to have some personal interaction with the individual to get a sense of what is going on.

Argumentative Personalities

Differences of opinions based on attitudes and perceptions often arise in group discussions. Remind the participants that disagreements are OK as long as they are handled in a respectful manner. Try to remain objective, listen to all sides, and look for the causes underlying the conflict. Irritability, withdrawal, and arguments typically are symptoms of defense mechanisms. The most important thing you can do is to deal with the issues. Your role is to help people look beyond their defenses so they can look at the situation objectively.

At one workshop, the facilitator had to deal with difficult behavior from a participant. As you read this case study, think how you might have handled the situation.

Case Study: The Power of One

One situation occurred with an intact workgroup composed of production workers in a manufacturing plant. The learning behavioral guidelines had been established and agreed on. After a less than stellar response to an introductory exercise, it was obvious that there was significant resistance to active participation by many of those in attendance. One participant was overtly verbal as to his lack of enthusiasm for the subject, and he seemed to wield strong informal influence on this intact group, although he was not a supervisor. While he was the most vocal about it, the sentiment also was somewhat visible on the faces of many of the other participants.

Case Resolution

Participants' distracting behaviors can range from complete nonparticipation, such as turning their chairs to face the back of the room, to verbally challenging any and every subject that is discussed. Although most challenges are not displayed to these extremes, how you manage these eventualities can take a potentially disruptive situation and create a learning opportunity for the participant(s) in question as well as the entire training group. It is important to remember that negative energy in the room can be transformed to positive energy if the needs of the participants are met and you actively consider and recognize the WIIFM on the part of the participants. Being dragged into a one-on-one discussion or debate does not serve the needs of the group. Rather than spend your time trying to convince or debate with an individual, turn such topics into open-ended questions addressed to the entire group in order to engage them and inform the discussion from sources in the room other than yourself.

Conclusion

Throughout your session it is important to model the behaviors you are teaching and discussing. Of the many ways to do that, one way is to make sure that your behavior as a facilitator models whatever behavioral guidelines you establish for your session. Another way is to make sure that participants also practice those behaviors. Finally, in the workshop itself, give participants the opportunity for reflective practices that support individual and team learning. One way of doing that is through the debrief questions asked at the end of each activity. For example, using the scenario above, a facilitator could ask,

- How did the discussion go at your individual tables?

- How were they different than other similar discussions you have had?

- What made the difference?

- How can we use this back in the workplace?

This sequence of questions encourages people to reflect on what they learned and consider how it relates back to the workplace.

Chapter 3
Getting to Know Each Other

We have become not a melting pot but a beautiful mosaic.
Different people, different beliefs, different yearnings,
different hopes, different dreams.

JIMMY CARTER

Participants come to workshops with different levels of knowledge and experience about diversity and inclusion. Some people may never have talked about this topic in a group; others may have had many conversations about it through church, community, friends, family, or work. However, your workshop or meeting will probably be the first time that this group of people has had the opportunity to talk and learn together.

Opening a diversity workshop with an icebreaker helps people get to know each other while exploring some aspect of similarities and differences among people. This approach has three primary benefits. First, participants practice having conversations that demonstrate they value diversity. Second, participants practice naming aspects of diversity in ways that are respectful and sometimes even playful and fun. Third, beginning with an activity that builds interpersonal connections among participants sets the stage for interesting and lively discussions later in your workshop.

This third benefit is very important. As the facilitator, your primary focus is on the learning of your participants. Finding activities and building sequences that encourage participants to explore, question, and actively engage with questions of diversity and inclusion that are relevant to them ensures that the session will be valuable for them as well as for you. This is part of what makes workshops and meetings unique opportunities for learning about ourselves as we relate to diversity and inclusion we get to interact and learn with others

This section presents activities you can use to begin building relationships among participants in ways related to diversity and inclusion.

Connections

Time: Basic Activity: 10–15 minutes   **Expanded Activity** e: 20–30 minutes

Equipment: Flipchart

Materials: Paper and a pencil or pen for each participant

Handouts: None

Objective:

■ To provide a simple introductory activity that helps participants identify commonalities

Procedure:

1. Ask participants to find a partner within the group, selecting a person they don't know well and preferably someone with whom they don't regularly interact.
2. Instruct the pairs to interview each other and to find out the things they have in common within 5 minutes. Ask them to record all of their commonalities as they identify them. Direct them to omit obvious commonalities like "We're both human," "We both work for this company," "We're both wearing clothes," and so on.
3. After 5 minutes, ask the pairs to stop making their lists.
4. Ask the participants to share with the rest of the group one commonality they discovered with their partners. Tell them every pair will have a chance to share at least one thing. Ask them not to repeat anything that has already been said when it is their turn. As they mention their commonalities, record them on the flipchart.
5. Tell the group that when they hear something mentioned that they have in common with the speaker, they are to call out the word, "connection."
6. Continue asking for input from each pair until all the commonalities have been identified.
7. Reconvene the large group and conclude the activity with the debriefing questions. If you are conducting the basic activity, stop after debriefing question 5. If you are conducting the expanded activity, ask all the questions.

Debriefing Questions:

1. What did you learn about each other?
2. How did you learn these things?
3. How does this relate to diversity?
4. How does this relate to building relationships?
5. How does this relate to building teams?
6. What can you take away from this activity
e 7. Why were we able to discover these things?
e 8. Why don't these things happen more often in the workplace?
e 9. What's required to create the sense of enough comfort and safety to be able to discuss and identify these things?
e 10. Do we make assumptions about people based upon what is observable? Why?
e 11. How does that impact our behavior and interactions with others?
e 12. How does that influence our performance and the performance of others?

Connections Continued

Key Points:

- Everyone has something in common with everyone else. Some of those things can be seen visually; however, most cannot.
- Communicating with each other allows us to discover more commonalities and points of connection. Appropriate relationships can be formed and enhanced through communication.
- We can begin to remove some of the barriers that separate people by identifying commonalities and seeing differences as having added value rather than as being wrong.
- Our personal experiences, values, and beliefs form the foundation of our reactions to the qualities we see in others. They influence whether we are initially drawn to and like a person, are initially repelled by or dislike someone, or sometimes have no reaction at all.
- By getting to know other people, we learn who they really are in contrast to our assumptions about them. This helps dispel preconceptions that would keep us divided—allowing us to align our energy and efforts to create stronger results and achieve common objectives.

Stats at a Glance

Time: Basic Activity: 20–30 minutes   **Expanded Activity** e : 30–40 minutes

Equipment: None

Materials: Trainer's Question and Answer Key: Stats at a Glance

Handouts: Statistics at a Glance

Objectives:

■ To give participants an opportunity to explore statistics relating to diversity in the U.S. workforce
■ To provide an opportunity for participants to be aware of what they already know
e ■ To give participants an opportunity to examine and compare U.S. and industry-specific diversity statistics with those of their organization

Procedure:

1. Divide participants into small groups of three to five people. Give each participant a copy of the handout titled "Statistics at a Glance."
2. Ask the small groups to go over each of the 11 questions and determine which answer is the most appropriate. The conclusions do not have to be unanimous. Allow 10 minutes.
3. Reconvene and review the questions with the entire group, point-by-point, first asking the participants for their answers and then offering the correct answers from the facilitator's answer sheet.

Debriefing Questions:

1. Of the statistics presented, which were most surprising or interesting? Why?
2. How do these statistics affect the organization?
3. How do these statistics affect your external customer base?
4. How might any of this information affect the way you carry out your work? What challenges or opportunities might you face? (Note: If you are using the Expanded Activity, this question should only be used to close the activity.)
e 5. What challenges or opportunities might your organization face?
e 6. What is your organization currently doing to be more diverse?
e 7. What is your organization currently doing to be more inclusive and appropriately leverage all diversity to meet and exceed business goals?
e 8. What more can your organization do to be more diverse? More inclusive?
e 9. What can you do to help create and sustain an inclusive environment?

Key Points:

■ People often have misconceptions involving diversity statistics.
■ The U.S. population and workforce are diverse and continue to become even more diverse.
e ■ While the diversity within the United States and its workforce may be increasing, that diversity may or may not be reflected within the organization.
e ■ When an organization is diverse, the diversity may be limited to certain positions within the organization. Employees who are different from the dominant culture may experience the phenomenon called the "glass ceiling."

Stats at a Glance **Trainer's Question and Answer Key**

Stats at a Glance Q & A Key

1. **More than 2,000 Americans were asked which groups of people they perceived as experiencing discrimination in the workplace, such as being fired, harassed, or denied a promotion. List the nine groups you believe they identified.**

   Answer:

Older adults (age 65 or older)	78 percent	Hispanic Americans	60 percent
Gays and lesbians	73 percent	Muslims	60 percent
People with disabilities	68 percent	Asian Americans	44 percent
Women	65 percent	Jews	39 percent
African Americans	61 percent		

2. **Which age group makes up the fastest-growing Internet population?**

   Answer: Baby Boomers and seniors

3. **Fill in the blank:**

   By the year 2006, more than 15 percent of the U.S. labor force will be ____.
   Answer: 55 years old or older

   By the year 2030, those in the workforce over ___ will double.
   Answer: age 55

4. **What terms are used to refer to the population born during the period 1981–2000?**

   Answer: Generation Y, Millennials, Nexters, Internet Generation

5. **What does the acronym GLBT stand for?**

   Answer: Gay, Lesbian, Bi-sexual and Transgender

6. **Among Americans age 70 years and older, there are 5.3 white people for every person of color or a ratio of five to one. For Americans below age 40, that ratio is two to one. What is the ration among children below age 10?**

   Answer: one and one-half to one *(Source: U.S. Census Bureau, 2000)*

7. **What is the largest minority subgroup in the United States?**

   Answer: People with disabilities (54 million people of all ethnic backgrounds, cultures, ages, and sexual orientations *(Source: Diversity, Inc.com)*

8. **White people are the majority population in ___ of the Nation's 100 largest cities?**
   Answer: 52

9. **In 1980, white people made up 80 percent of the population. What will that percentage be by the year 2040?**

   Answer: 50 percent *(Source: U.S. Census Bureau, (2000)*

10. **Asian and Pacific Islanders include people from what places of origin?**

    Answer: the Far East, Southeast Asia, the Indian subcontinent, or the Pacific Islands, including, for example, China, India, Japan, Korea, the Philippine Islands and Samoa *(Source: U.S. Census Bureau, (2000)*

Stats at a Glance Handout

Statistics at a Glance

1. More than 2000 Americans were asked which groups of people they perceived as experiencing discrimination in the workplace, such as being fired, harassed, or denied a promotion. List the nine groups you believe they identified.

2. Which age group makes up the fast-growing Internet population?

3. Fill in the blank:

   By the year 2006, more than 15 percent of the U.S. labor force will be _____ .

   By the year 2030, those in the workforce over _____ will double.

4. What terms are used to refer to the population born during the period 1981–2000?

5. What does the acronym GLBT stand for?

6. Among Americans age 70 and older, there are 5.3 white people for every person of color, or a ratio of five to one. For Americans below age 40, that ratio is two to one. What is the ratio among children below age 10 _____?

7. What is the largest minority subgroup in the United States?

8. White people are the majority population in _____ of the Nation's 100 largest cities?

9. In 1980, white people made up 80 percent of the population. What will that percentage be by the year 2040?

10. Asian and Pacific Islanders include people from what places of origin?

What's in a Name?

Time: Basic Activity: 20–30 minutes

Expanded Activity ⓔ: 40–60 minutes

Equipment: Flipchart

Materials: None

Handouts: What's in a Name?

Objectives:

- ■ To help participants recognize that each person has an identity and that a person's identity often begins with a name
- ■ To take a snapshot of diversity in the room through the lens of participants' names
- ■ To examine the effects of mispronouncing names
- ⓔ ■ To recognize that within some subcultures of the United States and in cultures outside the United States, names also may indicate or be associated with a person's position, occupation, economic status, or other social quality.

Procedure:

1. Ask participants to choose a partner, selecting a person they don't know well and preferably someone with whom they don't regularly interact.
2. Pass out the handout titled "What's in a Name."
3. Instruct the participants to use the questions on the handout to interview their partners. Tell them to take notes about pronunciation and facts so that they will be accurate when introducing their partners. Tell the pairs they will have 10 minutes to complete both interviews.
4. Ask the participants to introduce their partners to the large group.
ⓔ 5. Ask the participants to take a few minutes to answer the questions on the handout in preparation for introducing themselves to the group. They will introduce themselves using their answers to those questions. Allow 10 minutes for the participants to give their introductions.

Debriefing Questions:

1. What did you learn about each other?
2. What is the importance of names?
3. What is the impact of changing someone's name, for example by giving a nickname, shortening a name or Americanizing it?
4. What can get in the way of pronouncing someone's name correctly?
5. What can you take away from this activity? (Note: If you are using the Expanded Activity, this question should only be used to close the activity.)
ⓔ 6. How can not using someone's name correctly affect relationships and productivity?
ⓔ 7. Imagine that you just discovered that a new person has been hired to join your team by the name of Juan Martinez. What assumptions might pop up in your consciousness? What about other names, such as Sally White Eagle, Jane Smith, Larry Fitzgerald, Katherine Popovich, Lee Chang, Frederick Mandella? What are some of your reactions? Where do these reactions come from?
ⓔ 8. How might this automatic assumption response affect individual, team, and organizational effectiveness?
ⓔ 9. What can you do to become more aware of or offset those automatic assumptions?

What's in a Name? **Continued**

Key Points:

- Names are important to us. They are also one of many pieces of information we collect and use to form opinions and preconceived notions about people.

- Correctly pronouncing and using someone's name conveys an attitude of respect.

- Names are used in different ways in different cultures. In some places, a name is selected to honor an ancestor. In others, a name indicates a profession or position.

- When people introduce themselves using nicknames or derivatives of their names, they are usually giving us permission to use that name.

- When we give someone a nickname or change their name in some way, we may intend to create a sense of familiarity or camaraderie. Doing this may not, however, have the effect we intended. It is best to ask people what name they would like you to use when you introduce them or address them in daily interactions.

Trainer's Notes:

- Based on your own answers to the questions in the handout, introduce yourself to get the group started.

What's in a Name? **Handout**

What's in a Name?

Use the questions below to interview your partner. Then choose the information you will share with the large group in your partner introduction.

- Name (What is your name and how do you pronounce it?)
- Nickname (Do you have a different or more casual name? Do you or do you not want people to use that name for you at work?)
- Story (What's the story behind your name? Does it mean something or translate into words or actions? How did you get your name? Who gave it to you? Why?)
- Ethnicity (What is your ethnic or cultural background? Is there a naming tradition in your cultural background?)
- Personal History (What story from your family best represents your experience of your culture(s) and cultural identity?)

I Belong

Time: Basic Activity: 10–15 minutes   **Expanded Activity** e: 20–30 minutes

Equipment: None

Materials: None

Handouts: None

Objectives:

■ To acknowledge that people belong to many groups simultaneously
■ To better understand the diversity of the group in the session

Procedure:

1. Introduce the activity by saying, "Each person is a member of more than one group. Today we're going to identify some of the groups represented here. As I name a group, if you are a member, please stand up. The rest of us will acknowledge the group by applauding. At the end of the applause, please return to your seat."

2. Name groups such as people who

Only children	Card players	Married people
African Americans (over age 30)	Like to fish	White males
Went to parochial school	Women under 5'2"	Work with computers
Unemployed at least once	Had to uses crutches once	Parents both living

3. Invite the participants to propose additional groups. Tell them to continue standing if they are members of the group mentioned and to continue applauding each group.

4. After facilitating several rounds, begin the debriefing.

Debriefing Questions:

1. What is your reaction to this activity?

2. What did you observe? How did you feel and what did you think when you found you have so many things in common with the other people in this group?

3. What did you learn? How can you apply what you learned in the workplace?

4. Are there groups that people might not want to acknowledge they are members of? Why? Can you give examples?

5. How might it affect someone to feel that he or she must keep some aspect of his or her identity secret?

6. What can you do individually to increase inclusiveness?

e   7. What can we do to increase inclusiveness through our corporate policies, practices, and procedures?

8. What can you do individually to increase inclusiveness?

 **Continued**

Key Points:

- Some aspects of identity are visible. Many are not.
- Identifying commonalities and differences can be done quickly, and you can have fun doing it.
- Finding out what you do or do not have in common with someone and learning about their experiences deepens your understanding of that person. It helps you understand the other person's priorities and approach to decision-making.
- Even naming different categories helps identify assumptions that we commonly make. For example, by asking the people who are married to identify themselves, are we really asking who is in a committed relationship? Some people who are not married may consider themselves to be in committed relationships. How does sexual orientation enter into this category?

Trainer's Notes:

- An optional way of conducting this activity is to ask the participants to stand and form a comfortable circle. As groups are named, instruct people who belong to that group to go into the center of the circle, noticing who is inside the circle with them and who is not.
- This version of the activity tends to really energize the room and creates excitement and physical and emotional fun. As the activity picks up momentum, you'll probably find you don't have to call out categories, as the participants will quickly begin doing so with the slightest encouragement from you and. You also may have a challenge stopping the activity because it is so energizing and fun.
- For some groups or situations, you may want a quick way for people to identify subgroups represented in the room. Some categories you might include are
  - Ethnicity (South American, Asian, European, Native American, African American, Indian, Other)
  - Religion of birth (Catholic, Jewish, Protestant , Muslim, Buddhist, Hindu, Baha'i, Other)
  - Place of birth (East Coast, West Coast, Great Plains, the South, the Southwest, the Midwest, Outside of United States).

Name Tags R Us

Time: Basic Activity: 15–20 minutes   **Expanded Activity** ⒠: 20–30 minutes

Equipment: None

Materials: Prepared name tags for each participant

Handouts: None

Objective:

- To give participants a chance to meet one another and use specific topics to generate conversation while discovering similarities and differences.

Procedure:

1. Pass out prepared name tags to participants. Ask the participants to write their first names in the center of the tags and put them on.
2. Explain that the participants' task is to meet as many people as they can and, through conversation, discover similarities and differences. Tell them they can use any or all of the four words on the name tags as topics to generate discussions to find similarities and differences. Allow 10 to15 minutes for the conversation.
3. Reconvene the large group and conclude the activity with the debriefing. If you are using the basic activity, ask the first four debriefing questions. If you are using the expanded activity, ask all the questions.

Debriefing Questions:

1. What were your responses to this activity?
2. What kinds of questions did you find most helpful? Open-ended? Closed-ended? Why? What made you willing to share your answers with others?
3. What does this activity have to do with diversity and inclusiveness?
⒠ 4. Which categories were you most comfortable discussing? Why?
⒠ 5. Which were you most uncomfortable discussing? Why?
⒠ 6. How do you react when people begin or insist on discussing subjects that make you feel uncomfortable?
⒠ 7. What effect does avoiding or not talking about these things have on you, others, the organization, and productivity?
⒠ 8. What could be the effect of knowing you couldn't talk about or acknowledge some things that are important to you? What are some examples of those things?
⒠ 9. Is it beneficial to be able to discuss or acknowledge things that are important to us? What are the benefits? Who benefits?
⒠ 10. What must be in place so that everyone is comfortable discussing or acknowledging what is important to them? To others?

Key Points:

- We can learn some important things about each other quickly and we can have fun while doing it.
- Both commonalities and differences can be interesting.

Trainer's Notes:

- Prepare the nametags in advance, by writing the words "food," "travel," "family," and "hobbies" on the corners of each tag, as shown:

Food	Travel
Family	Hobbies

The History Channel

Time: Basic Activity: 30–40 minutes

Equipment: Flipchart

Materials: None

Handouts: About Me

Objective:

■ To educate each other about cultural differences and commonalities

Procedure:

1. Divide the participants into pairs. Explain that during the next 20 minutes they are to interview each other to find out their partner's name, how to pronounce it, and something about the person's cultural practices, observances, and priorities. Tell the participants to identify commonalities in what is done, how, and why. Where commonalities don't exist, the participants should ask questions that can help them understand the other person's culture. Tell them they will introduce their partner to the large group after the interviews are concluded.
2. Pass out and review the handout titled "About Me."
3. Tell the participants that they can choose a few other things to share with their partners about themselves and their cultures from the handout.
4. After 20 minutes, ask the participants to end the interviews. Ask each person to stand and briefly introduce his or her partner, beginning with the person's name and then summarizing what was discovered during the interview.
5. When each participant has had a chance to introduce and be introduced, conclude the activity by asking the debriefing questions.

Debriefing Questions:

1. What is your reaction to this activity?
2. How comfortable were you sharing?
3. How often do we share this kind of information about ourselves with others we work with?
4. What did you learn?

The History Channel Handout

About Me

Complete the following sentences and discuss your responses with your partner.

The culture(s) I primarily identify with are _____.

The way we introduce ourselves to others in professional settings is _____.

The way we introduce ourselves to others in social or family settings is _____.

To us, family includes _____.

Family is important because _____.

In my culture(s), it would be considered rude or I would be uncomfortable if _____

_____

_____

Choose one of the following topics for further discussion:
- Dress
- Food and eating customs
- Holidays and special occasions, including births, deaths, religious observances, and so forth (what and how they are acknowledged or celebrated)
- Gender roles

Chapter 4
Setting the Climate

To reach a port, we must sail—sail, not tie at anchor—sail, not drift.
FRANKLIN D. ROOSEVELT

People come to workshops and discussions about diversity with different kinds of experiences and sets of expectations. Creating a climate for learning includes establishing guidelines, the learning objectives, and the benefits for participants.

Establishing guidelines for the workshop means clarifying the behaviors expected during the session. Doing this creates a sense of safety for the group. For example, if confidentiality is one of the agreed-upon guidelines, participants may share more openly. If respect is another agreed-upon guideline, the guideline can be referred to if someone feels disrespected by a comment from another participant.

Establishing ways in which the objectives of the workshop or activity will benefit the participants also encourages participation. It is also important for facilitators to be clear about this in their own minds before selecting activities and designing a session. We have found that it can be helpful to link the learning objectives of the session to the mission, goals, and values of the organization.

This section presents activities you can use to create a climate for learning and establish ways that valuing diversity and building inclusiveness benefits organizations, employees, and customers.

When You C.A.R.E. Enough

Time: Basic Activity: 15–20 minutes   **Expanded Activity** e: 30–45 minutes

Equipment: Prepared flipchart

Materials: Paper and a pen or pencil for each participant.

Handout: When You Care Enough

Objectives:

- To have participants identify behaviors that support successful and meaningful diversity workshops, following the C.A.R.E. model
- To have participants explore ways of applying the C.A.R.E. model to the workplace

Procedure:

1. Present the C.A.R.E. model as it is described on the prepared flipchart.
2. Divide the large group into four smaller groups. Assign one letter or aspect of the C.A.R.E. model to each group. Ask the groups to develop a list of behaviors that demonstrate their assigned letter. Tell them to write their lists on the page(s) provided.
3. Instruct the small groups to select a reporter who will present their list to the full group. Give them 10 minutes to develop their list.
4. Reconvene the full group and ask each group to report out. As they do so, write the identified behaviors on the flipchart and tell the participants to fill out the appropriate areas on their sheets of paper.
5. Continue until all four groups have reported. Ask clarifying questions and encourage the participants to ask clarifying questions as they complete their own matrixes.
6. When all four groups have reported, tell the participants that they have created a list of the behaviors required to create a learning climate that will meet the objectives of the session. Practicing these behaviors also creates a climate of respect and appreciation.

Debriefing Questions:

1. Should any behaviors be added to the model? (If any behaviors are named, add them to the prepared flipchart.)
2. Are you willing to abide by these guidelines during the workshop?
3. Do I have your permission to give feedback on how well you are adhering to the guidelines throughout the session?

Key Points:

- When behavioral expectations are identified and agreed to, people create an environment in which they can do their best. Setting guidelines also sets the stage for accountability and feedback when the need arises.
- When we don't know the needs and expectations of others, we assume that their needs are the same as ours. This assumption works sometimes but creates problems at other times. Being explicit about expectations is the best procedure. Sometimes the Golden Rule works—treat others as you would like them to treat you. To create even more successful relationships, it is important to have the information we need to practice the Platinum Rule—treat others as they need or want to be treated.

When You C.A.R.E Enough **Continued**

Trainer's Notes:

- When group reports begin, ask the groups for permission to shorten what the reporters say so that you can write it concisely on the flipchart. Otherwise, use their exact words.

- Only add behaviors. Ask probing questions to help you discern the behavior if it is hidden beneath an assessment or judgment. For example, comments like "be professional" or "be kind" are not descriptions of actions; rather, they are interpretations of behavior. When participants suggest such phrases, follow up by asking questions like, "What do people who are being professional do?" or, "How do you know they're being professional?" "What do they do?"

- The guidelines you construct with your group become behavioral standards you can refer back to in the event that a participant says or does something that is outside of the spirit of valuing diversity. One way to do that is by directly saying, "We have a C.A.R.E. question here. Was what XX just said consistent with our list? Why? Why not?" Such an approach usually generates a valuable discussion and builds your credibility as a facilitator. Ignoring behavior that is out of the bounds of the behavioral guidelines you have established usually detracts from a session. In such an environment, participants may become less open as they feel less safe in contributing.

- An optional way of conducting this activity is to keep the participants in the large group and ask them to shout out additional behaviors after you have given several examples.

- Use the answers they provide to fill out the flipchart. Instruct the participants to write the additional behaviors on their handouts at the same time.

- Whether you use the basic or the advanced version of this activity, prepare the flipchart in advance, following the model shown.

The C.A.R.E. Model

Concern for Others. What do you want and need others to do to show they are considerate of you and your needs?

Examples: Listen, be honest without causing harm.

Appreciation. What do you want and need others to do to show they appreciate you and your participation, your questions and input, or your involvement and attention?

Examples: Say "Thank you." Reciprocate, sharing information with me as I am sharing with you.

Respect. What do you want and need others to do to show they respect you and your contributions in the workshop, to their learning about you, your culture, and what's important to you?

Examples: Acknowledge and validate some of my experiences if they are like or different from yours. Demonstrate body language that says you are listening and genuinely interested in what I'm saying.

Empathy. What do you want and need others to do to show they are empathetic?

Examples: Actively listen. Ask follow-up questions.

When You C.A.R.E Enough Handout

The C.A.R.E. Model

Concern for Others
Appreciation
Respect
Empathy

Why Diversity and Inclusion?

Time: Basic Activity: 30 minutes

Expanded Activity ⓔ: 45–60 minutes

Equipment: None

Materials: None

Handouts: None

Objectives:

■ To explore whether diversity and inclusiveness are issues of doing the right things or if they are smart business

■ To clarify how diversity and inclusiveness are linked to vision, mission, values, and goals of organizations, teams, and individuals

Procedure:

1. Define the terms *diversity* and *inclusiveness*
   ■ Diversity includes every aspect of a human being. It includes everything you know about a person by looking at them, such as their color, gender, height, and other physical characteristics, and it is also about things you can't see such as their personalities, religion, dominant hand, values, sexual orientation, where they live, their goals, and so on.
   ■ Inclusiveness is the act or process of using the information, tools, skills, insights, and other talents that each individual has to offer for the mutual benefit and gain of everyone. It also includes providing everyone with opportunities to contribute their thoughts, ideas, and concerns. Inclusiveness results in people feeling valued and respected. In addition, inclusiveness means that career development is available and encouraged to everyone. Note: If your organization has definitions of diversity and inclusiveness or of values intended to create diversity and inclusiveness, discuss them here.

2. Say, "In many organizations, there is some disagreement about whether diversity is predominately a fairness issue or business issue." To have the participants explore this matter further, divide the group into smaller discussion groups. Ask the groups to select a reporter.

3. Assign half the groups to discuss the pros and cons of the "fairness" argument. Assign the other half of the group to discuss the pros and cons of the "business" argument. Direct the recorders to capture the key points of their groups' discussion. Allow 10 minutes.

4. Reconvene the large group and ask for group reports. Write the points they bring up on the flipchart under the appropriate headings, "Fairness" or Business."

5. Lead the full group in a discussion by asking participants to comment on the points from the small group discussion. In the end, do they think that diversity is a fairness issue or a business issue?

6. Conclude with the debriefing questions. If you are conducting the basic activity, stop after question 5. If you are conducting the expanded activity, go through all the questions.

Why Diversity and Inclusion? Continued

Debriefing Questions:

1. Which is more important, "the right thing to do" or "smart business?" (The answer is: both.)
2. Why is it important to have an organization that is both diverse and inclusive?
3. How are diversity and inclusiveness linked with our organizational vision, mission, values, and goals?
4. How are they linked to your personal vision, mission, values, and goals?
5. What can you do to promote inclusiveness within your sphere of influence?
6. What best practices (systemic policies as well as behaviors) do we currently follow in our organization that value diversity and promote inclusiveness?
7. What opportunities do you see? What can we do to build on our current efforts and successes?

Key Points:

- Valuing diversity and creating inclusiveness are both the right things to do and smart business.
- The presence of diversity does not guarantee inclusiveness.
- Inclusiveness requires conscious decisions and actions. It is achieved by the presence, alignment, and demonstration of policies, procedures, and individual behavior.

Trainer's Notes:

- Participants may have questions about Equal Employment Opportunity and Affirmative Action. Review EEO and AA laws so that you are prepared.
- Note that valuing diversity means valuing everyone' uniqueness—including the uniqueness of white men. Too often, valuing diversity is perceived as valuing some types of diversity more than others. To create an inclusive organization, everyone must be included.

Treasure Hunt

Time: Basic Activity: 15–20 minutes   **Expanded Activity** e: 30–45 minutes

Equipment: None

Materials: None

Handouts: Treasure Hunt Fact Sheet

Objectives:

- To establish a positive climate for interaction
- To have participants discover and examine their similarities

Procedure:

1. Give each participant a copy of the handout titled "Treasure Hunt Fact Sheet."
2. Tell the participants to find descriptions that apply to them and then to initial the appropriate lines under the "Applies to Me" column. Tell them they can write in as many as two other things about themselves on the lines provided on the handout.
3. Ask the participants to circulate among the other group members and seek out someone they believe fits any of the categories they initialed. If the other person agrees that the category fits, he or she will initial the line for that category under "Applies to Others." The two participants will then separate and repeat the process with other people. If the other person does not agree that the category fits, no initialing will take place, and the two will separate and continue the process with other participants. Allow 5 to 10 minutes for the participants to gather the initials.
4. After 10 minutes, reconvene the large group.
5. After identifying all the things that apply to them, explain that this is an opportunity for participants to educate others by letting people know about something that they feel is important. Tell them to select one description that fits this category. During the next 20 minutes, they should talk with as many people as they can, sharing their own stories and collecting the stories of others. Tell the participants to write the full name of each person they talk to on the line in the "Applies to Others" column. Tell them to also write key words about the person's story to help them remember and be able to follow up if they wish to get more details later. After 20 minutes, reconvene the large group.
6. Conduct the debriefing. If you are conducting the expanded activity, go through all the debriefing questions.

Debriefing Questions:

1. What is your response to this activity?
2. What did you learn about others?
3. Which stories were most important to you? Why?
   e 4. How many of the things you learned did you know just by looking at one another?
   e 5. Why did you approach the people you did? What about them made them seem more approachable to you?
   e 6. What's the benefit of working with people who are approachable?
   e 7. What about people who don't demonstrate approachable behaviors, as you define them? What are the challenges of interacting with those people? What are the benefits? What can you do to overcome those challenges?
   e 8. What can you take away from this activity?

Treasure Hunt **Continued**

Key Points:

■ People share more similarities and commonalities than they realize.

■ You can identify similarities quickly.

■ It can be energizing to identify what you have in common with another person.

Treasure Hunt **Handout**

Treasure Hunt Fact Sheet

Description	Applies to Me	Applies to Others
A Baby-Boomer (born 1946–1964)		
Grew up on a farm		
Is an only child		
Has gone to the movies in the past two weeks		
Enjoys foreign films		
Has at least two friends or family members from different racial and cultural backgrounds		
Likes to cook ethnic food		
Likes to camp out		
Is a chocoholic		
Is multi-lingual		
Is a vegetarian		
Is an avid reader		
Takes off shoes before entering the house		
Performs routine service on own automobile		
Has one or more pets		
Oldest living relative is more than 80 years old		
Has had a recent birth in the family		
Has lived or worked in a country other than the U.S.A.		
Is an artist, musician, or writer		

Circle Game

Time: Basic Activity: 15–20 Minutes   **Expanded Activity** e : 30–40 minutes

Equipment: e Flipchart

Materials: None

Handouts: None

Objective:

■ To provide an experience that demonstrates how it feels to exclude and be excluded

Procedure:

1. Before separating the participants into small groups, ask for volunteers—one for each group—and instruct the volunteers to leave the room.
2. Depending on the size of the group, instruct the remaining participants to form one or more circles. Circles of five or six people are the most effective.
3. Explain to the group that the goal of each circle is to keep the volunteers from becoming part of their group. Tell them to come up with a strategy that will be effective in keeping others as outsiders and not allowing them to become members of the group. For example, instruct them to pick a subject and talk in a jovial, fun-loving manner. (A topic like planning a party or special event typically works well. Tell them they can use any verbal or nonverbal means possible to accomplish their goal *except* physical contact with the people who will be excluded.
4. Go out to the volunteers. Explain to the volunteers that, when they return, their goal is to become part of a group. Bring the volunteers into the room. Allow 5 minutes.
5. After 5 minutes, instruct all the participants to return to their seats for the debriefing process. Ask for a round of applause to thank the volunteers.
e 6. If you are conducting the expanded version of the activity, use the flipchart to record participants' responses to debriefing questions 9 through 16, which examine the topic in more depth as is relates to the participants' organization.

Debriefing Questions:

Ask the volunteers who were the outsiders:

1. How did it feel and what did you think when you were being excluded?
2. What did you do to try to be included?
3. After you weren't allowed to become part of the group, what did you begin to think or feel?

Ask the people who were insiders:

4. How did it feel and what did you think when you were excluding the volunteers?
5. What did you have to do to continue to exclude them?

Ask all the participants:

6. Does this kind of situation happen in the workplace?
7. What effect does it have on performance?
8. What can you take away from this activity?

Circle Game **Continued**

e Use the flipchart to record participants' responses to the following questions:

e 9. Who are the outsiders in the company you work for (if all belong to the same company or otherwise whatever company the participants are a part of)? Name titles, departments and groups of people. (Answers might include administrative staff, entry-level managers, finance, legal, long-term employees, college grads, Asians, and so forth.)

e 10. If these groups and people are allowed to continue feeling like outsiders, how will that affect their performance? (Review the list of things that the participants thought and felt about being excluded and treated as outsiders.) How will it affect the way they are perceived by others? Their motivation, enthusiasm, and loyalty?

e Ask the participants who were in the group, representing the insiders:

e 11. Who are the insiders within your organization?

e 12. What are the benefits of being an insider?

e 13. How does being insiders affect their performance? How are they perceived by others? How does it affect their motivation, enthusiasm, and loyalty?

e 14. Why did you exclude the outsiders? (They'll say because you told them to do so.) How much influence did my position as a facilitator have on your decision to exclude your peers?

e 15. Why additional reasons motivate people to exclude others? (Answers might include lack of relationship, stereotypes, assumptions, or group pressure and thinking.)

e Ask everyone:

e 16. What can you take away from this activity?

e 17. What can you do within your sphere of influence to create environments where everyone feels like and performs like insiders?

Key Points:

■ Inclusion and exclusion happens at all levels of the organization.

■ When people have to work hard to be included and heard, they have less motivation and energy to contribute their best effort.

■ Whether or not exclusion is intentional or conscious, the effects it has on those who are excluded are the same. A lack of intention does not lessen the effect of the behavior.

Trainer's Notes:

■ This activity works well regardless of the group's composition. If possible, when selecting volunteers, try to involve those who most likely have had the least experience in feeling excluded from a group.

Finding Commonalities

Time: Basic Activity: 15–20 minutes   **Expanded Activity** [e]: 30-40 minutes

Equipment: Flipchart

Materials: None

Handouts: [e] Finding Commonalities: Challenges and Solutions to Identifying Commonalities

Objectives:

- ■ To help participants understand that many commonalities can be identified when people look for them
- ■ To help participants understand that finding commonalities is an important step to bridging the gaps created by differences with others

Procedure:

1. Explain to the group that the goal of this activity is to have participants find people with whom they share the same values or background. The participants must find four commonalities, such as size of family, education, geographical roots, race, gender, responsibilities, or some other characteristic.
2. Instruct the participants to mill around the room and talk to as many people as possible in a 10-minute period.
3. After 10 minutes, reconvene the large group for the debriefing.

Debriefing Questions:

1. Who did you approach initially? Why?
2. Who found this activity to be easy? Why?
3. Who found this activity to be challenging? Why?
4. What did you think or how did you feel when you discovered you had something in common with another person in the group?
5. What can you take away from this activity? (Note: If you are using the Expanded Activity, this question should only be used to close the activity.)
[e] 6. What are the benefits in finding and discussing commonalities in the workplace with everyone?
[e] 7. What challenges do you face in finding and discussing commonalities with people in the workplace?
[e] 8. What can you do to overcome those challenges, particularly with people with whom you might find no—or perhaps only a few—commonalities?

Key Points:

- ■ Sometimes we don't realize how easy it is to exclude others when we don't share the same values, backgrounds, interests, hobbies, or goals.
- ■ Perceptions can differ from reality. We may assume that we have nothing or only insignificant things in common with others. Through discussion, however, we sometimes find this is not true.

Finding Commonalities **Continued**

Trainer's Notes:

- An optional way of conducting the expanded activity is to first identify and record challenges on a flipchart. Then divide the large group into smaller groups.

- Dividing the list of challenges among the small groups, give them 3 to 4 minutes to come up with solutions or strategies to overcome each assigned challenge. For example, if there are eight challenges, you might divide the large group into four small groups and assign two challenges to each small group.

- Then give the groups 6 to 8 minutes to develop solutions. Tell the small groups to select a reporter. Have each group present its recommendations to the larger group.

- If you choose this option, distribute the handout titled "Finding Commonalities: Challenges/Solutions to Identifying Commonalities" (as many sheets as possible) before the participants begin their small-group work, and direct the participants to use the handouts to focus and record their discussion.

Finding Commonalities **Handout**

Challenges/Solutions to Identifying Commonalities

Challenges	Solutions

Chapter 5
Personal Awareness

There are many paths to enlightenment. Be sure to take one with a heart.

LAO TZU

Our views of the world are shaped by many factors. Our individual cultural experiences and our cultural heritage are two important ones. Increasing our awareness about both of these aspects of our experience provides us with valuable information that helps us discover and understand the personal lens though which we see the world.

The term "culture" has many definitions. The definition we have found most helpful in our work is from the *Concise Columbia Encyclopedia* (Columbia University Press, 1994). It states: "Culture is the way of life of a given society, passed down from one generation to the next through learning and experience. It also includes language, values, communication styles, patterns of thinking, and norms of behavior."

Increasing our awareness about the cultural lens through which we see the world helps us discover when we are being unconsciously ethnocentric. The term ethnocentric refers to the attitude that one's own culture or group is superior to others. Sometimes this attitude reflects a kind of arrogance. Other times it results from sincere ignorance about other ways of doing things. Whatever the reason, ethnocentrism can be discovered at the moments when we, in face of a different way of doing something, automatically presume that our approach, interpretation, or opinion is the correct one.

It is very helpful to learn how to catch ourselves in moments of ethnocentrism because they offer us an opportunity to increase our awareness of the lens through which we see the world. Once our awareness has been raised, we can look again and decide consciously what response we want to make to immediate and long-term situations.

Being willing to catch ourselves being ethnocentric is essential to expanding our ability to value diversity and build inclusiveness. Without it, the best we can do is to tolerate people—and people who feel merely tolerated don't feel included. They know they are just being "put up with" and they will likely leave the organization or their morale will go down. When morale decreases, so does productivity. Such an outcome is not desirable for anyone—not for the person who feels tolerated and not for his or her team, manager, or organization.

This section presents activities designed to increase participants' awareness about their own cultural heritage and uniqueness and how it affects the lens through which they see the world and interact with others.

Decades on Parade

Time: Basic Activity: 20–30 minutes

Expanded Activity [e]: 45–60 minutes

Equipment: Flipchart

Materials: Paper and pens or pencils for participants

Handouts:

- Decades on Parade—Generational Events and Behaviors
- [e] Decades on Parade—Generational Attributes

Objectives:

- To help participants understand how they arrived at some of their values and current beliefs
- To recognize that many of the problems that occur between groups from different cultures in the workplace relate to early experiences

Procedure:

1. Tell the group that this activity focuses on events and people who were important in this country in each of the last five decades.
2. Divide the participants into five groups and ask them to assign a reporter who will present a summary of the group's discussion. Assign each small group a decade beginning with 1950.
3. Ask each group to jot down the first words they associate with people or events of their assigned decade. Allow 10 minutes.
4. Reconvene the large group and ask for the small-group reports.
[e] 5. Divide the participants into small groups of four or five people and distribute the handout for the expanded activity.
[e] 6. Tell the groups they have 20 minutes to assign the attributes listed on the first page of the handout into the correct generational category and list them under the appropriate generational category on page two. After 20 minutes, reconvene the large group and begin a general group discussion.

Debriefing Questions:

1. Based on the small-group reports, what decade had the greatest influence on you personally?
2. What impact did these did these early events and people have on the way you feel about diversity today? Your behaviors? Choices? Values?
3. How might the early events affect your relationships in the workplace?
4. What can you do to eliminate some challenges that may have been brought forward from your early tapes? Allow 15 minutes.
5. How do early tapes impact your workplace behavior? (Note: If you are using the Expanded Activity, this question should only be used to close the activity.)
[e] 6. What did you discuss with your tablemates?
[e] 7. What did you learn?
[e] 8. How did or do the influences, tapes, events, and people from your childhood affect what you think, feel, and believe about diversity today? Your behaviors? Choices? Values?
[e] 9. How might generational diversity affect relationships in the workplace?

From *Trainer's Diversity Source Book: 50 Ready-to-Use Activities from Icebreakers through Wrap Ups* by Jonamay Lambert and Selma Myers, © 2005, Society for Human Resource Management. All rights reserved.

Decades on Parade Continued

[e]   10. What can you do to build strong working relationships with people of all four generations described in the handout?

[e]   11. What can you do to eliminate the negative effects of any of your early tapes?

Key Points:

■ We all are affected by the time in history in which we were children and adolescents.

■ The term "early tapes" refers to the early words, phrases, concepts, and philosophies that influenced us during childhood or adolescence. These may be things that were expressed by others or things we personally discovered.

■ Our early tapes are hard to erase and impossible to erase without our being consciously aware of their existence and the full range of their impact.

Decades on Parade **Handout**

Generational Events and Behaviors

Sesame Street	Inclusion & Emphasis On Process	Straight Forward Cooperative Learning	Saving $	"We Value Your Experience"
Command Leadership	Use Credit	Personal Fulfillment	Civil Rights & Woman's Lib	Like On The Job Training & Development
Latch Key Kids	Loyalty To Family, Work, Country	Money & Career Advancement	Optimistic	Security & Comfortable Retirement
Game Boys	Consensual Leadership Style	60-Hour Work Week To Get Ahead	"If You Get The Job Done, Who Cares How You Do It."	Creative Ideas
Multiple Tasks	Persian Gulf War	AIDS	Duty	Government Disillusionment
"Think Globally"	Pessimistic	Directive	"You Are A Valuable Team Member"	Command & Control Leadership
Independent Worker	Delayed Reward	Cold War	Day Care	Fun & Spending $
Vietnam	Value Personal Fulfillment	Expect Diversity	Work When They Want	E-Mail
Korean War	Balance In Work & Life	Single Parent Homes	Techno Savvy	Respect Authority

Decades on Parade ⊜ Handout

Generational Attributes

Generation	Attributes
Veterans Born: 1922–1945	
Boomers Born: 1946–1960	
Gen X Born: 1961–1980	
Nexters (also known as Generation Y) Born: 1981–2000	

Cultural Introductions

Time: Basic Activity: 10–15 minutes   **Expanded Activity** ⌐e⌐: 30–45 minutes

Equipment: Flipchart

Materials: Paper and pen or pencil for each participant

Handouts: None

Objective:

- To help participants develop understanding, respect, and appreciation for their own culture and that of others

Procedure:

1. Divide the participants into small groups.
2. Ask the members of each group to introduce themselves to each other and share some aspect of their heritage and what it means to them. Tell them to consider what they are proud of or what makes them unique. (Note: If you are facilitating the Expanded Activity skip Step 3 and go directly to Step 4.)
3. Reconvene the large group and ask that one member of each group report on their discussion.
⌐e⌐ 4. After completing procedural steps 1 and 2 above, *do not* go to step 3. Instead, have each small group collectively develop a short, creative presentation that will introduce each culture represented in their group to the larger group. Encourage the use of skits, songs, poems, drawings, and so forth, and allow the groups to use the flipchart and any other tools, toys, or equipment that may be available to them in the room. Each member of the small group should take an active role in the presentation. Allow the groups 15 minutes to design their presentations.
⌐e⌐ 5. Reconvene and begin the group presentations, allowing approximately five minutes.

Debriefing Questions:

1. Why is culture important?
2. How much do you know about your cultural background?
3. How did you feel sharing information about your culture?
4. Are there aspects of your culture that you are particularly proud of? Not so proud of?
5. How can what you've learned help you in regard to diversity?
6. What can you take away from this activity?

Key Points:

- By sharing information about our culture with others, we remind ourselves of important things about our own cultures and important events in our lives.
- Not everyone can easily identify aspects of their culture.
- By allowing others to share information about their cultures with us, we learn or confirm information about their cultures that can help us build and enhance relationships with them and others who share their cultural heritage.

Choices

Time: Basic Activity: 10–15 minutes   **Expanded Activity** e: 20–30 minutes

Equipment: None

Materials: None

Handouts: None

Objective:

- To experience factors and dynamics that demonstrate how individuals decide whom to include (when choosing people to work with)

Procedure:

1. Ask the group to stand up and walk around the room as if they were at a reception or cocktail party.
2. Give the following instructions:
   - Each person's goal is to form a work group of four or five people. To do that, your task is to find individuals with similar histories, values, attitudes, work and family responsibilities, and even assumptions about other people.
   - After you have met one or two participants who share things in common with you, identify and establish criteria for others to join. For example, your group may find that you are all single parents who are concerned about childcare. Perhaps you attended the same high school, enjoy the same hobby, or are active in specific social advocacy programs. As the criteria become fixed, allow only those people who match the established criteria to join your group.
3. Reconvene the large group and conclude the activity by asking the debriefing questions

Debriefing Questions:

1. How did you feel during this activity?
2. Was it easy or difficult?
3. Were there any surprises?
4. What factors entered into your decisions about whom to talk with?
5. If you were one of the people who were included, what did you think and how did you feel when you were included?
6. What did you think about yourself and the group you joined?
7. If you were one of the people who were excluded, what did you think and how did you feel when you were excluded?
8. What did you think about yourself and the group you weren't allowed to join?
9. How does this activity reflect what happens in the real world of work and community?
10. What can you take away from this activity? (Note: If you are using the Expanded Activity, this question should only be used to close the activity.)
- e 11. What are the benefits of working with people with whom you have things in common?
- e 12. What are the potential pitfalls of only working with people with whom you have things in common?
- e 13. What are the benefits of working with people who are different or with whom you have little (or don't know what you have) in common?

Choices **Continued**

14. What one or two things can you do, within your sphere of influence, to create a more consistently inclusive environment at work? Identify the one or two actions and set timelines for each of them.

15. Have participants share their action plans and timelines with either one other person in the room or with everyone at their table to create accountability and to share ideas.

Key Points:

■ When people have a choice about the people with whom they will work, they may try to find people with whom they have more similarities than differences.

■ We may unintentionally exclude people without intending or realizing it.

■ Our choices affect who we invite or are willing to allow on our teams, in our organizations, and even in our customer base.

■ As we strive to broaden our knowledge, economic, and global bases, we must continue to invite people with whom we have immediate connections—but we also must begin to invite those with whom we do not.

Sharing Cultural Stories, Legends & Tales

Time: Basic Activity: 15–20 minutes   **Expanded Activity** e: 30–40 minutes

Equipment: None

Materials: None

Handouts: None

Objective:

■ To explore diversity by having participants share cultural stories, legends, and folktales

Procedure:

1. Divide the participants into pairs or small groups. Ask each person to think of a specific story, legend, folktale, or myth from his or her own culture.

2. Have the participants spend the next few minutes telling each other their stories. It is all right if the stories happen to be the same.

3. Next, have the participants discuss the stories. Ask them to consider any similarities and differences.

4. Reconvene the large group and have the participants briefly report on their discussions.

5. Discuss any generalizations that can be drawn from this activity.

e 6. After a few minutes, ask the participants to find a partner, preferably someone who does not work in their department or team. Have the sharing partners discuss their goals, timelines, anticipated challenges, and ways to overcome them. Tell the listening partners to ask clarifying questions, suggest missing steps in the action plan, and offer alternative solutions for your partner's issues. Allow 15 minutes to share goals and timelines.

Debriefing Questions:

1. What is your reaction to this activity?

2. Did you find stories, legends, or folktales that are the same or similar in different cultures? What are they?

3. What does having similar stories tell you about diversity?

e 4. How do we make decisions about what information we share about ourselves with others? What influences our decision as to what is appropriate to share and discuss at work? In our personal lives?

e 5. What topics or information would be helpful for us to know about others? Why would these topics or information be helpful to us? To them? To the organization? To our external customers?

e 6. What qualities or elements increase our comfort with sharing information about ourselves?

e 7. What specific behaviors encourage openness?

e 8. What specific behaviors discourage openness?

e 9. What can you do within your sphere of influence to create an environment in which everyone is encouraged to share information about themselves?

e 10. Identify one or two people who might share more information if you created or enhanced an environment to make people feel safer in sharing.

e 11. What challenges do you face in reaching this goal?

e 12. What can you do to overcome the challenge(s)?

Choices Continued

e 13. What will you do to create or enhance the environment between you? Set a timeline for beginning your strategy and process.

14. After the skill practice ends, reconvene the group. Ask "What can you take away from this activity and apply in the work-
e   place? In your personal life?

Key Points:

■ Every culture has stories, legends, and folktales. Many such stories are similar and cross cultural boundaries.

■ By understanding each other's cultures, we begin to understand each other.

■ Cultural stories can serve as a bridge to establish commonalities and to overcome barriers.

Trainer's Notes:

■ Besides stories or folktales, you can also ask participants to discuss objects or symbols that represent their cultures.

Close Encounters of the First Kind

Time: Basic Activity: 30 minutes

Equipment: Flipchart

Materials: None

Handouts: Close Encounters of the First Kind

Objective:

■ To help participants explore the diversity of their contacts with people who are different from them in age, gender, ability, religion, and so forth

Procedure:

1. Begin with questions to the group about what they see as various kinds or categories of diversity, referring to words like "race," "ethnicity," "religion," "age," "sexual orientation," and so on. As the participants call out words, write them on the flipchart.
2. Pass out the handout titled "Close Encounters of the First Kind" and ask the participants to jot down answers to the first two points in the "Dimension of Diversity" column.
3. Ask the participants to pair up with a person sitting near them and compare their responses. Allow a few minutes, and then tell them to return to their individual handouts and fill out the "Current Diversity Contacts" on the second half of the sheet. Note the first line as an example.
4. After 15 minutes, reconvene the large group and conclude the activity by asking the debriefing questions.

Debriefing Questions:

1. How did the place where you grew up affect the kinds of diversity contacts you made? How?
2. What messages did you receive about other people or groups that were different from you?
3. What messages did you receive about people who were like you?
4. How do diversity contacts differ between your business life and your personal life?
5. What specific experiences with diversity have been most outstanding or memorable? Why?
6. How can your experiences with, and intelligence about, diversity benefit you in your professional life? In your personal life?

Key Points:

■ The number of contacts between people of diverse cultural groups is generally quite different in social situations than in work situations.
■ No matter what the context is in which we develop our understanding of the dimensions of diversity, we can leverage our experiences and contacts to better succeed in our interactions with others.

Close Encounters of the First Kind

Answer the questions and fill in the blanks:

1. Where did you grow up? Describe the location and any other pertinent information.

   _____

   _____

   _____

   _____

   _____

   _____

2. What were your earliest experiences with diversity?

   _____

   _____

   _____

   _____

   _____

   _____

3. My diversity contacts: In the first column below, list the dimension of diversity (kind or category of diversity) that you have had experience or contact with. In the second column, describe any or all of your experiences or contacts at work with this dimension of diversity. In the third column, do the same in relation to your personal life. In the last column, write any comments about how you have built or will build or leverage this experience or contact so that you can increase your knowledge and awareness and create more inclusiveness at work.

Dimension of Diversity	Work Life	Personal Life	Comments
1.			
2.			
3.			
4.			
5.			

Knee-Jerk Response

Time: Basic Activity: 15–20 minutes   **Expanded Activity** **e**: 40–50 minutes

Equipment: Prepared flipchart

Materials: Notepaper and a pen or pencil for each participant

Handouts: None

Objectives:

- To show how simple phrases may affect people differently and create different responses
- To identify our conscious and unconscious "hot buttons" and resultant behavior that may create barriers to relationship building
- To identify ways to choose to respond or behave appropriately when your personal hot buttons are pushed

Procedure:

1. Ask the participants to list 1 through 10 down the side of their sheets of paper. Explain that you will read out, one at a time, 10 phrases with a diversity slant. Without giving the matter any thought, they should immediately write "positive," "negative," or "no opinion" as their response to that phrase next to the appropriate number. For this activity, the trainer can make up any 10 phrases.
   - Some suggestions are
   - Persons with a strong French accent
   - Bowing when acknowledging others
   - Old people
   - Foreign food colors
   - Songs whose lyrics you don't understand (opera or rap, for example)
   - Non-traditional clothing (turbans, oversized religious accessories, yarmulkes or other hats worn indoors, and so forth)
   - Persons with a strong Spanish accent
   - Disabled persons who move slowly
   - Other cultures' holidays, fiestas, and celebrations
   - People who use words like "Boy," "Girl," "Honey," or "Babe"
2. Read the phrases one at a time, and have the participants silently raise their hands for "positive," "negative," or "no opinion." Using a prepared flipchart that has the numbers 1 to 10 written in a column on the left and three additional columns headed "positive," "negative," and "no opinion," ask for and record the number of answers in each column for each phrase.
3. Lead a discussion examining the differences in responses to each phrase.
4. **e** Ask the participants to identify two or more of their hot buttons and write them on a blank sheet.
5. **e** Direct the participants to form groups of four or five people and designate a reporter for their group.
6. **e** Ask the participants to share their two hot buttons. Then ask them to identify three ways they can tell when each hot button has been triggered and what they can do to avoid falling into the assumption trap. Allow 20 minutes.
7. **e** After 20 minutes, have one reporter present one challenge and its three identified solutions. Then ask if anyone else has solutions for this one challenge.
8. **e** Go to the next table and repeat the process. Continue in this fashion until all challenges have been shared and solutions recommended by every table.

Knee-Jerk Response **Continued**

Debriefing Questions:

1. What are your responses to this activity?
2. Why do some people respond positively, some negatively, and some not at all to the same statement or issue?
3. Why might it be helpful to identify and test assumptions before taking action? How do you do this?
4. What can you take away from this activity to apply so that you are more successful managing your hot buttons in the workplace?

Key Points:

■ Many factors shape our knee-jerk responses to information or situations, including our previous experiences, cultural stereotypes, personalities, and more.

■ Those knee-jerk responses happen in a split second and often create barriers to building or enhancing relationships with people who are different from us in some way.

Chapter 6
Values

There never was in the world two opinions alike, no more than two hairs or two grains; the most universal quality is diversity.

MONTAIGNE, *OF THE RESEMBLANCE OF CHILDREN TO THEIR FATHERS*

Our values are shaped by many factors, including cultural background, personality style, preferences, and personal experiences. These are some of the forces that shape the lens through which we see, perceive, and judge all of our experience. They affect our decisions about the information we take in and the actions we take at work and at home.

Our values help us select the sources of information we think are credible and the kinds of information we think we need to know. Some mechanism for doing this is essential in a world where we can easily be overwhelmed by information. Consider sitting in front of a television set that receives a hundred channels. We can't watch all the channels at once. As we flip through the options with a remote control, our values help us decide which programs we will pass by, and which programs we will watch. In a similar way, as we go through life, our values help us decide what information we will collect and remember. Along with other factors, our values help create filters that keep some information out of our awareness.

Once we have information, our values affect the actions we take at home and at work. For example, values influence our on-the-spot decisions about whom we talk to at lunch, in the airport, or in the grocery store. They influence the way we assign projects, lead teams, and participate in groups. They influence our decisions about whom we are willing to mentor or whom we ask to mentor us. The list goes on and on. The actions that result from these decisions affect our social environment, enhancing or reducing inclusiveness in various settings, including at work or in community organizations.

This section presents activities you can use to increase your awareness of your own and others' values and how values influence decision-making and behavior.

Values, Values, Values

Time: Basic Activity: 30–40 minutes   **Expanded Activity** e: 40–60 minutes

Equipment: Flipchart, e prepared flipchart

Materials: Paper and a pencil or pen for each participant

Handouts: None

Objective:

■ To give participants an opportunity to identify and examine their own values and to learn what others value

Procedure:

1. Tell the participants, "Your home is on fire. You have time to choose five things you can take with you and escape to safety. All other things will perish in the flames, and you won't be able to replace them. If you take the time to choose more than five things, you and the five things you choose will all perish. Your choices can include animate and inanimate objects, individuals or groups of people, pets, and anything else you choose. In this scenario you have 5 minutes. What will you take with you?"

2. Ask the participants to write their lists of five things. While they are thinking of their choices, write the following discussion questions on a flipchart page:
   ■ What items did you take and why?
   ■ What do they mean to you individually and/or collectively?
   ■ Why are they more important than the things you left behind?

3. After 5 minutes, put the participants into pairs.

4. Tell the pairs they have 10 minutes to share their lists and discuss them using the questions posted on the flipchart as a guide to the discussion. Post the flipchart page you have just prepared.

5. If you are doing the basic activity, reconvene the large group after 10 minutes and proceed to the debriefing questions.

e 6. Tell the participants they will now have an opportunity to further clarify their values. Ask, "If you could take only one of the five items, knowing that the other four will perish, what would you choose to take with you?"

e 7. Reveal the prepared flipchart labeled "Values and Choices." Direct the participants to work in their pairs again to discuss their answers in relation to the questions on the flipchart. Say, "Consider these additional questions:
   ■ Why did you choose this one item?
   ■ What benefits do you realize? What are the positive things you receive by having this one item?
   ■ What would you lose if you had to give up this one item? How would that impact you and your life?
   ■ How would not having the other four items impact you and your life?
   ■ How would your choice affect you and your life? How would it influence your behavior and interactions with others? Your performance?"

e 8. After 7 minutes, reconvene the large group and conclude the activity by going through the debriefing questions.

Debriefing Questions:

1. Who found making the decision of what to take and what to leave behind easy? Why?
2. Who found it difficult? Why?
3. What influenced your decision-making? (What cultural beliefs, people, events, and needs influenced you? How?)
4. What did you learn about what is important to you? (What did you learn about what you value most at this time in your life?)

Values, Values, Values **Continued**

5. As you listened to your partners, what did you learn about them? What were the similarities and differences in your choice of values?

6. What were some key things you and your partner discussed?

7. How does this activity apply to diversity?

8. What can you take away from this activity? (Note: If you are using the Expanded Activity, this question should only be used to close the activity.)

[e] 9. What did you learn about what you value most at this time in your life?

[e] 10. What have you learned about discussing values with others?

Key Points:

■ Relating values to diversity is important because values affect business decisions as well as choices in our everyday lives. While everyone has values, they vary from person to person and from culture to culture.

■ Our values represent what is important to us. Being able to live in ways that are congruent with our values contributes to our satisfaction, our quality of life, and our ability to contribute our best.

■ Our values are influenced by our culture, including family, peers, nation, religion, education, experiences, and so forth.

Trainer's Notes:

■ If you will conduct the expanded activity, keep the prepared flipchart page covered until you are ready to reveal the additional questions.

■ If you will be writing the questions for the first part of the activity during the session itself, you may want to post the prepared flipchart page for the expanded activity in advance, covering it with a blank sheet until it is needed. This will prevent having ink accidentally "bleed through" onto the prepared flipchart page while you are writing.

■ If you prefer to keep the prepared page on the flipchart itself, be sure that several sheets of blank paper shield it from the page you will be writing on. Alternatively, you may wish to prepare flipchart pages with both sets of questions in advance, keeping the pages covered until you need them.

Values, Values, Values ⓔ **Prepared Flipchart**

Values and Choices
1. Why did you choose this one item? ■ What benefits do you realize? ■ What positive things do you receive by valuing this one item? ■ How would your choice affect you and your life? 2. What would you lose if you had to give up this one valued item? How would that choice affect you and your life? 3. How would not having the other four valued items affect you and your life? 4. How would your values and choices influence your behavior and interactions with others? Your performance?

Million-Dollar Question

Time: Basic Activity: 15 minutes

Expanded Activity ⓔ: 30 minutes

Equipment: None

Materials: Blank paper for the basic activity

Handouts: ⓔ Million-dollar Planning Guide

Objective:

- ■ To give participants an opportunity to clarify the personal values that influence the choices they make

Procedure:

1. Ask the participants the following question: If you were given $1 million, what would you do?
2. Divide the participants into groups of three or four people. Instruct each group to appoint a reporter to summarize the group's decisions.
3. Tell the participants they don't have to agree on what they would do with the money, but should make a list that includes all the things that everyone in the group says. Allow 10 minutes.
4. After 10 minutes have passed, reconvene the large group and ask for the small-group summaries. Following the summaries, if you are doing the basic activity only, proceed to the debriefing questions.
ⓔ 5. Direct the participants to consider their values and goals. Say, "Look at your group's list and identify the items that would be on your personal list." Allow 3 minutes.
ⓔ 6. Tell the participants to organize their lists in rank order according to what they would most like to do.
ⓔ 7. Direct the participants to review their ranked lists. Ask, "What could you do right now with a million dollars?" Allow 3 minutes.
ⓔ 8. Pass out the handout titled "Million-dollar Planning Guide." Instruct the participants to write down their answers to the questions on the handout. Allow 3 to 5 minutes.
ⓔ 9. Say, "Consider the following series of questions. As I ask the questions, write what first comes to mind. Allow yourself to answer the questions honestly. No one will see what you have written."
    - ■ Question 1: What internal or external barriers have prevented you from doing the top two or three items on your list?
    - ■ Question 2: What am I gaining by not doing this?
    - ■ Question 3: What am I losing by not doing this?
    - ■ Question 4: What will I gain by doing this?
    - ■ Question 5: What will I lose by doing this?
    - ■ Question 6: What action plan might you implement to accomplish those top two items? You might not be able to do the whole thing, but is there something you could do that would chip away at one of those goals and positively affect your life?
ⓔ 10. Reconvene the large group and have each group's spokesperson report out.

Million-Dollar Question **Continued**

Debriefing Questions:

1. Were there any surprises?
2. How similar were the responses from the different groups?
3. Was this activity easy or difficult?
4. What did you learn about yourself? About your team? About others?
5. What would you think and feel about your life if you did the things you have identified to reach your goals?

Key Points:

- Everyone comes to the workplace with values that influence goals and priorities.
- Values are determined by people's experiences as well as cultural influences.
- These personal values influence the way we explore and see various options
- The way we see these various options in turn affects the choices we make
- The more we know about other people and their values, the easier it is to find ways of working effectively towards a common goal.

Million-Dollar Question ⓔ **Handout**

The Million-Dollar Planning Guide

What one to three items from your prioritized list will make the most immediate and positive difference in your personal and professional life? Write those items in the spaces provided below for Goals #1, #2, and #3. For each goal, list what you will do in the next 3 days, 3 weeks, and 3 months to make the goal a reality.

Goal #1: _____

_____

_____

_____

In the next 3 days, I will…

In the next 3 weeks, I will…

In the next 3 months, I will…

Goal #2: _____

_____

_____

_____

In the next 3 days, I will…

In the next 3 weeks, I will…

In the next 3 months, I will…

Goal #3: _____

_____

_____

_____

In the next 3 days, I will…

In the next 3 weeks, I will…

In the next 3 months, I will…

Use the space below to write in your thoughts in preparation to the questions posed by your facilitator.

Additional Thoughts: _____

_____

_____

_____

Value Line

Time: Basic Activity: 15–20 minutes   **Expanded Activity** e : 30–40 minutes

Equipment: None

Materials: None

Handouts: None

Objectives:

- To provide participants an opportunity to identify their own values and understand value differences
- To offer greater insight into the effects of culture on individuals, their biases, and their assumptions
- To identify challenges and benefits that differences bring to problem solving

Procedure:

1. Ask participants to define values. (See Trainer's Notes)
2. Instruct the participants to stand up and form a single line facing you.
3. Give the following instructions: "I am going to call out two values. Depending on which word matches the value that you hold, you are going to move to one side of the room or the other. If you are uncertain which is most important, you will stay in the middle. We will address one set of values at a time."
4. Using the sets of values listed in the Trainer's Notes, announce which side of the room the participants will move to for each set. For example, you could say, "The two values are money and power. If you value money more than power, move to the left side of the room. If you value power more than money, move to the right side of the room. If you are unsure, say in the middle of the room."
5. After calling out the first pair of values, have the participants on each side of the room discuss how they feel about the people who selected the opposing value. In other words, ask the group that chose money over power how they feel about the group that chose power. Likewise, ask the group that chose power over money how they feel about the group that chose money. Then ask both groups how they feel about the people who did not make a choice and stayed in the middle. Ask the people who stayed in the middle how they feel about the groups that chose sides.
6. Repeat the above process, reinforcing the instructions after you call out each set of values. Call out as many sets of values as you feel appropriate.
7. Have the participants return to their seats. If you are conducting the basic activity, conclude with the first five debriefing questions. If you are conducting the expanded activity, ask all of the debriefing questions.

Debriefing Questions:

1. What do you think and how do you feel about this activity?
2. Where do values come from?
3. What did you think and feel about what was said about your group?
4. Were there any surprises?
5. What did you learn?
6. What can you take away from this activity? (Note: If you are using the Expanded Activity, this question should only be used to close the activity.)
   e   7. What assumptions did you make about the people who stood with you?

Value Line Continued

8. What assumptions did you make about the people who made the other choices?

9. Which choice is the "right" one? Which is more important than the other?

10. What are the challenges in interacting respectfully and inclusively with people whose values differ from yours?

11. Are there challenges in interacting respectfully and inclusively with people who share the same values as you? What are they?

12. What can you do to overcome and eliminate the challenges and barriers of communicating with people who don't share your values? With people who do?

13. What are the benefits of respecting differing values and beliefs in the workplace?

Key Points:

- Research indicates that we form 90 percent of our values by age 10, and because these values often reflect the way we grow up they are not easy to change.

- Each person comes to work with a unique set of personal principles based on his or her early life experiences and cultural background.

- Because values influence behaviors in the workplace, it is imperative to remember that all people do not think alike, nor do they value the same things.

- 1) Respect for others and 2) appreciation that differences bring an expanded set of ideas are two concepts that are essential for productive exchanges of information when it comes to problem solving. Sometimes opposing choices may present themselves as sources of frustration or actually may have a negative impact within your organization.

- Values are defined as principles (personal life guidelines or ground rules) that are believed in and are held in high esteem
  - Values are shaped by a person's cultural background.

- Values differ based on personal experiences.

- Values are one of the elements that make up the lens through which we see, evaluate, and judge experiences.

Trainer's Notes:

- Values are defined as principles (personal life guidelines or ground rules) that are believed in and are held in high esteem.

Sets of Values		
Money	vs.	Power
Security	vs.	Risk
Conformity	vs.	Nonconformity
Climbing the corporate ladder	vs.	Family coming first
Individualistic	vs.	Group-oriented
Respect from others	vs.	Self-respect
Leadership	vs.	Following the group
Control	vs.	Delegation
Competition	vs.	Cooperation
Long-term	vs.	Short-term
Practical application	vs.	Cutting-edge technology
Force	vs.	Persuasion

Trading Value Cards

Time: Basic Activity: 15–20 minutes   **Expanded Activity** **e**: 20–30 minutes

Equipment: **e** Prepared flipchart

Materials: 3" x 5" index cards, each with a value from the value template sheet (see Trainer's Notes). Prepare enough cards to distribute five cards, including at least one wild card, to each participant.

Handouts: None

Objectives:

- To give participants an opportunity to learn more about their own values as well as those of others
e ■ To give participants an opportunity to experience being forced to choose between values that are important to them

Procedure:

1. Explain that the objective of the activity is to trade value cards until participants have collected only cards that represent their personal values.
2. Pass out five index cards to each participant. Make sure each participant gets at least 1 wild card. Explain that the wild card becomes any value they want it to be. Tell them their goal is to try to obtain cards that most closely represent their own values. They will obtain cards by trading, one-for-one, any of their cards that they feel don't best reflect their values. Encourage the participants to talk to people near them or even to walk around and talk to other participants.
3. Explain that if a participant is unable to make a trade with one trading partner, he or she can move on to another one. Begin the trading process and allow 5 to 10 minutes.
4. Reconvene the group and go over the results, using the following debriefing questions.
   - What was the hardest value to obtain? The easiest?
   - What was the hardest value to trade off? The easiest?
   - What were the values about which you felt the most strongly?
   - What have you learned about values?
   - What did you learn about yourself? How will you apply these learning at work?
e 5. After the participants have exchanged cards with one another, instruct them to go to the side or back table to see if they can make an even better exchange with some of the cards there. Let them know they can only have 3 value cards in their hands by the time they are done.
e 6. Divide group into small discussion groups and answer the questions listed on the prepared flipchart.
   - How have your values changed in priority or meaning over time?
   - How did you know they had changed? What events propelled the changed and/or your recognition that they had changed?
   - If you had to give up these values, how would it impact your professional life? Your personal life?
   - What can you do to more fully integrate your values into your professional life? Your personal life?

Debriefing Questions:

1. What's your response to this activity?
2. What were some of the challenges that you faced?
3. How do you feel when someone doesn't respect what you consider to be positive aspects of your culture?

Trading Value Cards **Continued**

4. How do our values affect our attitudes, behaviors, and choices?
5. What can you take away from this activity?

Key Points:

- We all have values.
- Whether we are conscious of what our values are or not, they influence our behaviors, attitudes, and choices.
- If or when we do not embrace our values, our frustration level increases and our satisfaction and happiness levels decrease.
- Over time and with the occurrence of life changing events, our values may change substantially.
- There are many benefits to periodically inventorying our values and examining how we are incorporating them into our lives.

Trainer's Notes:

- Using the value templates below, cut out enough cards so that each participant can have five cards (including at least one wild card) to begin with.
- Laminate the cards so you'll be able to use them again with other groups of participants.
- For the expanded version, make and laminate an additional 20 to 30 value cards ahead of time. Place the additional value cards on a table at the back or side of the room.
- Write the following questions on flipchart paper:
  - How have your values changed in priority or meaning over time?
  - How did you know they had changed? What events propelled the changes or your recognition that your values had changed?
  - If you had to give up these values, how would it affect your professional life? Your personal life?
  - How might you more fully integrate your values into your professional life? Your personal life?
  - What action plan might help you to do that?

Trading Value Cards **Instruction Sheet and Templates**

Trading Value Cards Instructions and Templates

Make 10 copies of the Value Cards from the templates below. If you choose to recycle the Values Cards, laminate them after cutting them into cards. Shuffle the cut cards; then distribute five cards to each participant. Add or change the list of values to create valuable discussions during the debriefing. You also may want to include your organization's values.

Achievement	Advancement & Promotion	Adventure
Affection (Love & Caring)	Change	Competence
Competition	Cooperation	Creativity
Family	Freedom	Helping Others
Honesty	Independence	Inner Harmony
Integrity	Knowledge	Leadership
Loyalty	Nature	Order/Structure
Personal Development	Power	Privacy
Punctuality	Religion	Reputation/Esteem
Responsibility	Serenity	Sophistication
Spirituality	Stability	Status
Truth	Wealth	Wisdom
Wild Card	Wild Card	Wild Card
Wild Card	Wild Card	Wild Card
Wild Card	Wild Card	Wild Card
Wild Card	Wild Card	Wild Card

Chapter 7
Assumptions and Stereotypes

*A great many people think they are thinking
when they are merely rearranging their prejudices.*
WILLIAM JAMES

One exciting aspect of exploring diversity is that it offers us a direct opportunity to examine our mental maps of the world. These maps are the pictures, thoughts, and assumptions that we carry in our minds about ourselves, each other, and the world. We all need ways to define and describe our world and the people in it, but these maps—also described as mental models—are not always accurate.

Because our mental models exist below our conscious awareness, we are not aware of them most of the time and do not often test or challenge them. A good diversity session allows participants to examine their models and talk about them with minimal defensiveness. And participants can test whether their models are accurate, see the effects of their thinking, and, if appropriate, form new models that are more accurate and constructive.

Peter Senge, in *The Fifth Discipline Fieldbook*, presented a Ladder of Inference to describe how individuals form their mental models. Using Senge's Ladder as a starting point, here is how a person would describe the building of his or her model:

1. I choose data that are observable and based on experiences;

2. I overlay my personal meaning on top of these experiences or data;

3. I make assumptions based on the meaning that I attached;

4. I do not challenge my assumptions;

5. I reach a conclusion, which becomes a belief;

6. Once I have a belief about something, that belief affects how I perceive similar situations; and

7. I act based on what I believe.

A mental model developed this way and never challenged can easily lead to misguided beliefs that affect both our actions and our perceptions. With this information as a backdrop, we have found that it is often useful to have at hand working definitions for the following words, which often come up in diversity workshops:

- Assumptions.

- Beliefs.

- Discrimination.

- Generalizations.

- Perception.

- Prejudice.

- Stereotypes.

Assumptions are suppositions that a statement or conclusion is true without verification. Assumptions also may apply to situations.

Beliefs are ideas held as facts and thought to be true without any knowledge or proof.

Discrimination is the act of denying opportunities, resources, or access to a person because of his or her group membership. Discrimination can take many forms including racism, sexism, ageism, heterosexism, able-ism, and so forth. It is prejudice (see below) in action.

Generalizations are general statements that are usually true and are made about a group of people. Such statements are understood to be often true of people in the group, but not necessarily true for everyone included in the group.

Perception has several meanings. It is the awareness of the elements of environment through physical sensation. It is also a physical sensation interpreted in the light of experience. The term also refers to the ability to discern, sort, and interpret data.

Prejudice is a preconceived idea, most often a negative attitude taken before the facts are known and sustained by overgeneralizations. Prejudice reflects a bias without reason that resists all evidence to the contrary. Prejudice implies inferiority, leads to suspicion, and is detrimental to communication and interpersonal relationships.

Stereotypes are exaggerated beliefs or fixed ideas about a person or a group that are held by a number of people and sustained by selective perception and selective forgetting. Stereotypes arise from incomplete or distorted information and limited experience. They often come from outside sources, such as others' interpretation of cultural behavior. Stereotypes reflect human nature but often are destructive because they are unfair, do not allow individuality, and interfere with communication.

This section presents activities you can use to increase awareness about assumptions and stereotypes that affect us consciously and unconsciously. These activities also can help us explore what we can do about such attitudes.

What Does it Mean to You?

Time: Basic Activity: 15 minutes   **Expanded Activity** e: 30 minutes

Equipment: None

Materials: e Pictures

Handout: What Does It Mean To You?

Trainer's Worksheet: What Does It Mean to You? Suggested Words and Phrases

Objective:

■ To bring attention to the fact that people relate to, define, and experience events and situations differently, depending on their culture, background, expectations, and other factors

Procedure:

1. Distribute a copy of the handout titled "What Does It Mean to You?" to each participant.
2. Divide the group into small groups of three to four people. Mix the participants by age, gender, and other dimensions of diversity as much as possible.
3. Tell the participants you are going to read a series of words and phrases to them. Ask them to write the word or phrase in the left-hand column of the handout and what it means to them in the right-hand column.
4. Read five words or phrases from the trainer's worksheet.
5. Give the participants time to write their responses.
6. Ask the participants to share and discuss how they each defined the words or phrases. Give them 10 minutes; then conclude the activity with the debriefing questions.

Debriefing Questions:

1. What did you discuss in your groups?
2. Were there words or phrases that everyone defined the same way? If so, which ones?
3. Were any differences of opinion anchored in some version of what is right versus what is wrong? How did those discussions go? What helped? What didn't help?
4. What links do you make between experience, perception, and opinions?
5. What can you take from this activity and apply to your daily work life? (Note: If you are using the Expanded Activity, this question should only be used to close the activity.)
e 6. Consider your overall discussion as we continue our debriefing with some questions designed to further examine your small-group discussions:
    ■ Using a scale of 1 to 5, where a rating of 1 means that the group's discussion had a constructive "listen to understand" tone and a rating of 5 means that the group's discussion was characterized more by talking at each other than listening to each other, how would you rate your conversation?
    ■ Why did you rate your group's discussion the way you did?
    ■ What behaviors did you observe?
    ■ How did your group's discussion affect you?
e 7. In what ways and in what circumstances is it useful to discuss differences in perceptions, opinions, or expectations? Consider possible benefits to you, your team, and your organization. What helps? What gets in the way? What can you do?

What Does it Mean to You? Continued

Key Points:

■ Often we argue about "truth" without fully appreciating the extent to which truth can be relative. What is true for one person may not be true for another.

■ Our past experiences and external influences influence our perceptions all the time as we make moment-to-moment assessments of the world and people around us.

■ Often things are not what they appear to be. Usually it is very helpful to be aware of the assumptions embedded in our judgments and assessments.

■ Individuals, teams, organizations, and outside stakeholders benefit when people are able to share, understand, and learn from one another's experiences and "truths." This ability is central to harnessing the power of diversity. Working constructively with differences usually takes us out of our comfort zones, but it usually results in a stronger product or outcome. It also sets the stage for future success as it promotes greater inclusion on the next project or effort.

Trainer's Notes:

■ An optional way of conducting this activity is to prepare handout with words and phrases already written in the left-hand column so that the participants can do the activity in silence and only write in what each word or phrase means to them.

What Does it Mean to You? Trainer's Worksheet

Suggested Words and Phrases

Direct the participants to write the following words and phrases in the left-hand column of their handouts, and to write their definitions for the words and phrases in the right-hand column.

1. Career
2. Discipline
3. Diversity
4. Entertainment
5. Family
6. Loyalty
7. Personal fulfillment (What is personally fulfilling to you?)
8. Security
9. Work ethic

Direct the participants to write down what first comes to mind to complete each of the following phrases:

1. People primarily communicate through_____.
2. My favorite TV show is_____.
3. The news event that I best remember is _____.
4. The most favorite movie star of all time is _____.
5. The most popular coffee is _____.
6. President _____.
7. World War _____.

What Does it Mean to You? **Handout**

What Does it Mean to You?

Word or Phrase:	My Definition or First Response:
1.	
2.	
3.	
4.	
5.	
6.	
7.	
8.	
9.	
10.	
11.	
12.	
13.	
14.	
15.	
16.	

Do You See What I See?

Time: Basic Activity: 10–15 minutes   **Expanded Activity** e: 20–30 minutes

Equipment: Overhead Projector

Materials:

- Pictures (overhead transparencies, PowerPoint slides, or handouts)
- Paper and a pen or pencil for each participant

Handouts: Do You See What I See

Objectives:

- To bring attention to the fact that people relate to, define, and experience events and situations differently depending on their culture, background, expectations, and other factors
- To increase awareness about the automatic reactions we have to situations and people we encounter
- To clarify that while we don't necessarily have control over those automatic reactions, we do have control over how we respond to them

Procedure:

1. Collect pictures from magazines or clipart to show using PowerPoint slides, overhead transparencies, or handouts. Collect pictures of single people, couples (men, women, mixed gender), people of different ages, races, and so forth. Note: If the team or organization has little experience with diversity or difficulty including people from all groups, be sure to include pictures showing dimensions of diversity that will best challenge and educate participants.
2. Pass out the handout titled "Do You See What I See?"
3. Ask the participants to use the handout to write down the first reactions—both thoughts and feelings—that they notice in response to what they see.
4. Show one picture at a time. Show three to seven pictures
5. Divide the large group into discussion groups of four to five people. Appoint a reporter for each group.
6. Remind the participants that it is okay to not share their automatic reactions if they prefer. Ask participants to share, as they are willing, the automatic reactions that came up after seeing each picture. What assumptions did participants make about the people in the photographs in terms of their
   - Professions
   - Ages
   - Family status
   - Formal education
   - Where they live
   - Favorite music
   - Favorite food
   - Any other assumptions that came up.
7. Reconvene the large group and wrap up the activity using the debriefing questions.

Do You See What I See? **Continued**

Debriefing Questions:

1. What stood out from your small-group discussion? What surprised you? What did you learn?
2. What was the basis of the assumptions that shaped your reactions?
3. Were there many similarities or differences among the reactions in your group?
4. How quickly are first impressions made?
5. Who can share an example of a time when someone made an assumption about you? What was the effect?
6. What can you take away from this activity? (Note: If you are using the Expanded Activity, this question should be only used to close the activity.)
7. What challenges do you face in the workplace because of assumptions made about others? What challenges to you face in the workplace because of assumptions made about you?
8. How do assumptions about you affect your behavior in the workplace? The behavior of others?
9. What can you do to overcome those challenges?

Key Points:

- First impressions usually are made within 1 to 5 seconds. They influence what we notice, how we value others, and how we interact with them.
- First impressions are influenced by our assumptions and the biases that have been shaped by our experiences and the messages we have received about the world through the people in our lives and various media we watch, listen to, or read.
- Whether our impressions and perceptions are wrong or right, in the workplace, we must find ways of working together to achieve common goals.

Do You See What I See? Handout

Do You See What I See?

After each picture you see, please write down the very first thoughts and feelings that you notice. No one will see what you have written. You will be discussing your responses with your group, but what you share will be optional. Please just jot down what comes into your mind.

	Visual	First Reaction(s)
1.	_____	_____
2.	_____	_____
3.	_____	_____
4.	_____	_____
5.	_____	_____
6.	_____	_____
7.	_____	_____

One Potato, Two Potato

Time: Basic Activity: 15 minutes

Equipment: None

Materials:

- Raw potatoes, one for each participant
- Aluminum foil
- Container

Handouts: None

Objectives:

- To examine ways in which careful observation can help a person's performance, noting that the more observant a person is the more effective he or she can be

Procedure:

1. Ask the participants to come to the front of the room, select one of the foil-wrapped potatoes from the container, and return to their seats with it. (See Trainer's Notes for pre-session instructions.)
2. Explain that everyone has a raw potato and that the assignment is to unwrap the foil, study the potato, and become familiar enough with it to describe its unique features to someone else. Allow a few minutes for this part of the activity. (The aluminum foil can be discarded.)
3. Put the participants in small groups and ask each person to introduce his or her potato by describing it. Allow 5 minutes.
4. Gather up all the potatoes and put them back in the container in a random fashion.
5. Ask each of the groups to come to the front of the room and see if the participants can identify their own potatoes. Invite the participants to take their identified potatoes with them at the end of the activity.

Debriefing Questions:

1. What's your reaction to this activity?
2. What did you learn about the process of observation?
3. Were there any surprises?
4. How can you apply this experience to the topic of diversity?

Key Points:

- People have the capacity to distinguish between objects that seem to be very similar.
- This same concept can be applied to diversity. Members of groups of diverse peoples are not all exactly alike. Through careful observation, a person can readily pick out significant differences among individuals, even in an unfamiliar group or team.
- By looking for and acknowledging both similarities and differences between and among others and ourselves, we can begin to gather information that can serve as a foundation for respect, valuing, and inclusion.

Trainer's Notes:

Prepare ahead of time by wrapping each potato in aluminum foil and placing it in the container. This activity can also work with other objects, such as rocks and apples.

Even Exchange

Time: Basic Activity: 30 minutes

Equipment: None

Materials: None

Handouts: None

Objectives:

- To help participants gain greater self-awareness
- To identify similarities and differences among group members

Procedure, Round #1:

1. Divide the group in half. Ask one half to stand on the left side of the room and the other half to stand on the right side.
2. Ask the participants who are standing on the right side to look at the participants on the left side and choose the person that they believe might be the most similar to themselves. Tell them that once they've made their selection, they should go to that person and discuss why they made the choice they did. Allow 5 minutes for the participants to complete these steps.
4. After the 5 minutes have passed, tell the participant pairs to talk to each other in order to discover something they do not have in common—a difference between them. Allow 5 minutes for this step.
5. Ask the participants to return to their seats. Conclude this part of the activity by going through the debriefing questions for both rounds.

Procedure, Round #2:

1. Repeat Step #1 from the first procedure.
2. Repeat Step #2. This time, however, ask participants on the left side to choose someone they believe might be the most unlike themselves.
3. Once they've selected the person they believe to be most unlike themselves, instruct them to go talk to that person to find something they have in common.
4. After 5 minutes of discussing similarities, ask them to talk about some of their differences.
5. After 5 minutes more, ask the participants to return to their seats. Conclude this part of the activity by going through all of the debriefing questions.

Debriefing Questions for Round #1 and Round #2:

What did you discover you and your partner have in common?

What did you discover are some of your differences?

How difficult was it to find the commonalities?

How difficult was it to find the differences?

Did you find it easier or more difficult to talk about commonalities or differences? If so, why?

Additional Debriefing Questions for Round #2 Only

What does this activity have to do with the topic of diversity?

How can you apply what you've learned back in the workplace?

Even Exchange **Continued**

Key Points:

■ Some of our similarities and differences are obvious. Others cannot be seen.

■ We often make choices and decisions based on what we see.

■ By investing the time to get to know someone, we discover other similarities and differences. This knowledge can be leveraged to demonstrate respect, promote creativity, achieve common goals, and so on.

ZAP Model

Time: Basic Activity: 15–25 minutes

Equipment: Flipchart

Materials: None

Handouts: Applying the ZAP Model

Objectives:

- To encourage participants to identify a stereotype that influences their behavior
- To practice and discuss ways of disarming the influence of a stereotype

Procedure:

1. Remind the participants that we all are influenced by stereotypes. No one is immune to them. The key question is how effective are we at knowing when we are seeing a person or a situation as it really is versus when we are seeing that person or situation in terms of a stereotype. A related question is "How do we work with ourselves to disarm such stereotypes so we can think and act more effectively?"

2. Say that in this activity participants will get to practice working with the ZAP Model. The ZAP Model offers one kind of antidote to the influence of stereotypes.

3. Ask the participants to identify a stereotype that they know influences them in some way that creates a challenge for them. Explain the ZAP Model by talking about how you have used it to deal with a stereotype that has influenced you and that has made you feel uncomfortable. Suggest that the participants follow the ZAP Model on the flipchart and jot down their responses to the model. (See Trainer's Notes.)

4. Distribute the handout titled "Applying the ZAP Model" and give the participants a chance to complete it.

5. Divide the group into pairs. Ask the pairs to discuss the stereotypes they chose and what they learned by applying the ZAP Model.

6. Suggest that the participants' discussion include the source of the stereotype and what they can do to counteract its negative effect. Encourage them to arrive at some examples of people or behavior that can counteract the stereotypes they chose.

7. Reconvene the group. Ask for volunteers to share some examples of what to do to counteract stereotypes. Record the responses on a flipchart page labeled "Ways to Effectively Challenge and Discount Stereotypes."

Debriefing Questions:

1. What have you learned or confirmed about stereotypes and stereotyping?

2. What actions or strategies did you identify that you can use to challenge, change, or eliminate stereotypes?

3. How does stereotyping affect individual performance? Team performance?

4. Do some groups quickly bring forth a stereotype when they are mentioned? Note for trainer: Encourage participants to look at all levels of the organization for groups that might be stereotyped.

5. What can you do to challenge, change, or eliminate stereotypes within your sphere of influence?

ZAP Model **Continued**

Key Points:

- Stereotyping occurs both consciously and unconsciously. It is something that everyone does.
- Instead of feeling badly about being influenced by stereotypes and trying to act as if we aren't affected by them, it can be helpful to get curious about them and want to understand more about where they come from, how they get reinforced, and what we can do to reduce their ability to influence or affect us personally.
- It is helpful to learn to detect signs of our own stereotype-based thinking so that we can raise it to our conscious awareness and eventually eliminate its impact on us.

Trainer's Notes:

- Be sure to have an example of using the ZAP Model to share with participants.
- Before the activity begins, write the steps outlined on the handout on the flipchart as talking points for your introduction to the activity.

ZAP Model **Handout**

Applying the ZAP Model

Follow each of the steps below.

1. Zero in on a stereotype that negatively influences you that you would like to work with.

2. What do you know about where this stereotype comes from? How is it reinforced now?

3. In what ways does this stereotype influence you and your behavior? How do you feel about its influence?

4. What would it be like if you could reduce the influence of this stereotype? How would it benefit you? Would it benefit others? Who? How?

5. What examples of people or behavior can you think of that counteract the stereotype? If you can't think of any, how might you go about getting that sort of information?

6. How might you respond next time this stereotype pops up? What might you say to yourself? How might you behave differently?

What about Positive Stereotypes?

Time: Basic Activity: 10-15 minutes   **Expanded Activity** e: 15-20 minutes

Equipment: Flipchart with definition of the word stereotype (See Trainer's Notes.)

Materials: None

Handouts: None

Objectives:

- To discuss stereotypes and whether there can be positive stereotypes
- To discuss how stereotypes in general affect behavior at work

Procedure:

1. Begin by asking the participants to define the word *stereotype*, encouraging them to describe what the word means to them.
2. Explain to the group that sometimes people believe that stereotyping is okay if the words used are positive. For example, sometimes one hears words like "smart," "hardworking," "good athlete." and so forth, or sentences such as "Asian children are good at math" or "women are good with dealing with feelings," or "Latinos are hardworking." Ask participants for their thoughts and feelings about this notion of positive stereotypes.
e 3. Make the statement that all stereotypes are limiting, restrictive, and unfair.

Debriefing Questions:

1. What happens to your relationship when your experience of the other person is influenced by a stereotype? Does it make a difference if the stereotype is positive or negative? If yes, what is the difference? If no, why not?
2. How does stereotyping affect performance?
3. How does stereotyping affect employees' willingness to work together?
4. What did you learn that you can apply in your workplace? (Note: If you are using the Expanded Activity, this question should only be used to close the activity.)
e 5. If all stereotypes are limiting, restrictive, and unfair, why do you think this is so?
e 6. How does stereotyping affect employees' willingness to include everyone and their ideas?
e 7. How does stereotyping affect a company's bottom line? The overall environment?
e 8. What can you do to overcome, change, and eliminate stereotyping?

Key Points:

- Stereotypes are one factor that shapes the lens through which we perceive others. In turn, that lens shapes our behavior and expectations.
- All stereotypes are limiting and restrictive, whether they are intended to be positive or negative. They keep us from getting to know another person as he or she really is.

Trainer's Notes:

- *Webster's Third New International Dictionary* (Merriam-Webster Inc., 2002) defines the term *stereotype* as "A standardized mental picture held in common by members of a group and representing an oversimplified opinion, affective attitude, or uncritical judgment (as of a person, a race, an issue, or an event)."

Checking Assumptions Scenario

Time: Basic Activity: 15–20 minutes   **Expanded Activity e:** 25–30 minutes

Equipment: None

Materials: None

Handouts: Scenario

Objectives:

- To examine the effects of assumptions on performance, interactions, and demonstration of respect toward others
- To explore the potential impact of unchecked assumptions on individuals, teams, and organizations

Procedure:

1. Set up discussion groups of four or five participants and have each group select a reporter.
2. Pass out copies of the handout titled "Scenario" to all participants and allow them a few minutes to read it.
3. Ask the small groups to discuss the scenario using the questions provided in the handout. Ask them to write their answers on a piece of flipchart paper for presentation to the large group. Allow about 10 minutes.
4. Reconvene the large group and ask reporters to review the flipchart that summarizes their groups' responses.

Debriefing Questions:

1. What did you discuss in your group?
2. Does this happen in the real world?
3. What does this have to do with diversity?
4. What can you take away from this activity?
e 5. When things like this happen, how could they affect the relationship between Zachary and Rachel? How about on relationships between Zachary and others who overhear the conversation he had with the customer and then Rachel?
e 6. What might the customer be thinking about their organization? Do you think the customer will remain their customer? How about his or her family and friends?
e 7. What is the overall impact of this kind of exchange on our bottom line?
e 8. How might such an interaction affect our jobs and our stability as an organization?

Key Points:

- Excellent customer service is not a good idea; it is an imperative for organizations that want to survive. Customers can be internal to the organization (a colleague who relies on us to produce a deliverable that she uses to produce her deliverable) or external (someone who purchases the ultimate product or service of the organization.). Excellent service is critically important whether you are dealing with internal or external customers.
- Silence or a failure to respond to a situation where diversity is not respected creates the perception that the behavior is acceptable. What it really means is that no one spoke up to disagree or give feedback. When such situations occur, they usually have some effect on both the person who spoke and the people who heard what was said.
- We all are informal leaders, regardless of our position or title. Each person contributes to creating a positive climate that encourages excellence from everyone. Too often it is easy to think that someone else should do something instead of taking whatever action we can to influence a situation—especially when taking action takes us out of our comfort zone. At the same time, change often happens one person at a time. Each of us makes a difference.

Checking Assumptions

Zachary and Rachel work at the customer relations desk. The workload has been hectic, and they are scrambling to keep up. Zachary picks up the next call, which is from a male customer with a heavy foreign accent. The customer appears to be describing an unsatisfactory situation, but Zachary can't understand what he's trying to say.

Annoyed and frustrated, Zachary finally breaks in, saying, "I really can't figure out what you're trying to tell me. Why don't you ask someone who speaks English to call in for you?" The customer hangs up.

Zachary then says to Rachel, "He doesn't know what he's talking about. I wish people like him were smarter and could learn to speak English so we could understand them. After all, they're in our country. My grandfather came over and he learned to speak English. People like this guy should either learn our language or go back where they came from."

Questions for Small-Group Discussion:

1. What's happening here?
2. What assumptions did Zachary make?
3. What could he have done differently?
4. What, if anything, should Rachel do or say?
5. How might behavior like Zachary's affect the company?

I See, You See … Changing Lenses

Time: Basic Activity: 10–15 minutes

Expanded Activity e: 20–30 minutes

Equipment: None

Materials: Two very different pairs of eyeglasses

Handouts: None

Objectives:

- To experience how our assumptions influence our perceptions and how our perceptions in turn influence our assumptions, creating a self-reinforcing cycle
- To demonstrate the power of assumptions based on limited information

Procedure:

1. Hold up one pair of eyeglasses. Ask the participants to describe the characteristics of the person they feel would have worn that pair of glasses.
2. Hold up a second pair of eyeglasses of a very different style, color, and so forth. Ask participants the same question.
3. Describe the people who wore the glasses. (Here you can either describe the actual person or create a description that will make the point that it's easy to make assumptions that are often incorrect.)

Debriefing Questions:

1. How long did it take you to begin to form the stories about the people who wore these glasses?
2. Did you ask questions to find out what was true before you began to form the stories?
3. How does this activity relate to day-to-day life?
4. What can you take away from this activity?
5. **e** How do our perceptions and assumptions about others affect our behavior toward them?
6. **e** What examples can you think of where someone made an incorrect assumption about you or someone you care about? What effect did it have on you? What did you think and feel about the person who made the assumption(s)? What, if anything, did you do? How did your actions impact your relationship with the person?
7. **e** If this was a work situation, how was your performance affected?
8. **e** What does this have to do with diversity?

Key Points:

- First impressions, which are usually made within 1 to 5 seconds, affect what we see, think, and believe about others and influence our behavior toward them.
- It often is difficult to change a first impression once it has been made.
- People can be "pigeon-holed" into certain positions because others cannot get beyond how they see that individual.
- Unless someone or a situation challenges our assumptions, we usually remain unaware of our first impressions and continue to think that they reflect "how it is." We remain unconsciously unaware of what we don't know. (See the Chapter Introduction for more information on this kind of situation.)

Chapter 8
Communication

Honest difference of views and honest debate are not disunity.
They are the vital process of policy among free men.
HERBERT CLARK HOOVER

Communication is perhaps the most important diversity skill. Without it there is no way to get to know a colleague or solve a conflict. The greater the span of diversity, the more important it is to be able to communicate effectively. Communication is the glue that keeps the organization or a team together.

Communication happens in various ways—face-to-face, over the telephone, in an e-mail or a video announcement, to name but a few. Despite the advent of the electronic age, we still track a lot of communication though nonverbal signals, such as body language, facial expressions, and tone of voice.

Proactively, effective communication skills help get relationships off to a positive start. Reactively, effective communication skills help us in negative feedback situations—whether we are giving the feedback or receiving it. They are also, of course essential when turning a difficult conflict situation into a constructive exchange.

It is important to communicate what we mean to say in some way that ensures that the effect of our communication is congruent with our intention. It also is important to know what questions to ask and then to listen to the responses we get. Listening goes beyond hearing the words. It includes paying attention to the nonverbal communications as much if not more than the words. While there are times when it is easy to listen, there are certainly times when it is difficult, as when we don't agree with the person who is speaking or when we have piles of stuff to get through on our desks. At those times—especially at those times—it is important to listen carefully to the other person.

We benefit from effective communication skills in at least three ways when it is time to problem-solve. First, we will likely be working to solve the right problem. Second, the solutions developed may be more innovative in response to our clear understanding of the problem. Third, the people we listen to will feel heard and, as a result, feel valued, which will strengthen both work relationships and personal relationships.

Key skills to good listening include:

- Asking questions that deepen understanding of the other's perspective and experience;

- Being willing and able to set our internal self-talk aside; and

- Being willing to be influenced by what we hear.

Culture influences communication skills and styles. For example, the Japanese language has no translation for the English word "no." As a result, if a non-Japanese person is asking someone from Japan to do something, it is important to listen carefully to the response. If that person answers with "That would be very difficult," this may be the person's way of saying "no." Someone from the United States might interpret such as response to mean "It could be done if we figure out some way to overcome the challenges."

Differences in the way language is used and perceived can create difficulties in either personal or business contexts. For example, an organization that is very hierarchical is likely to have staff meetings where employees are given direction and their input is rarely sought when managers make decisions. The top-down culture is likely to influence communication in ways that profoundly affect the business in many ways.

Cultural and organizational norms affect behavior as well as verbal communication. In the case of Japan, the lack of the word "no" in the language is linked to norms of interaction and valuing harmony. In the case of the hierarchical organization, it is likely that little informal interaction takes place between people at different levels of the company. This lack of interaction may have the effect that people don't get promoted much or that important information available at the hands-on level of the organization doesn't get taken into consideration in decision-making.

This section presents activities you can use to examine aspects of communication that help build relationships and increase understanding when working in any situation—especially ones where dimensions of diversity are a factor.

Nonverbal Introduction

Time: Basic Activity: 10–15 minutes   **Expanded Activity** ⓔ: 20–30 minutes

Equipment: None

Materials: None

Handouts: None

Objectives:

- To explore ways in which information is communicated without words
- To explore the impact of nonverbal communication

Procedure:

1. Organize the group into pairs and ask them to stand facing each other.
2. Explain that this activity will be done without using words. Instruct the participants to introduce themselves to each other in any way they wish but without using words. This includes no use of American Sign Language, "silent speaking," or using writing implements. Allow about 5 minutes.
3. Bring the participants' attention back to the large group and ask pairs to introduce their partners, this time using words, based on the information they gathered in the nonverbal exchange.
4. Lead a discussion using the debriefing questions.
ⓔ 5. For the extended activity, refer to the additional information covered in the Trainer's Notes and ask the participants the additional debriefing questions.

Debriefing Questions:

1. What was it like to do this activity?
2. How well did your partner introduce you? What did you learn about your nonverbal communication as a result of what was said?
3. How did you choose what to communicate about yourself in the first part of this activity?
4. What did you discover about yourself?
5. What did you learn about your partner?
6. How does this activity relate to valuing diversity?
7. What can you take away from this activity?
ⓔ 8. Remembering that communication takes place through three primary channels—words, vocal tone and pace, and visual cues such as body language—which of the three channels do you think has the strongest impact? What is the basis for your answer? (See the Trainer's Notes.)
ⓔ 9. What examples of body language promote positive interaction within your culture? Are they different from the body language that builds relationship and trust in mainstream U.S. culture, such as handshakes, eye contact, close proximity or personal space, and so on?

Nonverbal Introduction Continued

Key Points:

■ We communicate information about ourselves, including our attitudes, feelings, and thoughts, all the time. No words are required.

■ At the same time, we receive and track information about each other all the time.

■ We often underestimate the potency of nonverbal communication; it actually makes up 93 percent of communication.

■ Paying attention to nonverbal signals from someone we are talking with is an essential part of tracking the effect of our words. If we notice cues that indicate discomfort or disconnection, we can then respond, adjust our communication, or explore the causes for the discomfort. Closely monitoring nonverbal cues helps us make sure that in the end, the effect of our communication is congruent with our intention.

■ Remembering that communication is strongly influenced by culture, working with cultural diversity increases the importance of paying attention to all nonverbal cues—both the ones that we send out and the ones that we perceive from others.

■ Other aspects of diversity (such as personality, work style, and role or position) are also important factors in effective communication.

Trainer's Notes:

■ Sometimes participants challenge the idea that nonverbal communication has a strong impact. A helpful illustration of the power of nonverbal communication is to say a phrase two times using the exact same words but using different tones of voice and body language.

■ You also can ask participants if they have been in a situation where the words in a message were very clear but the body language was out of sync with those words. Usually you will get nods or other indications of "yes."

■ Follow up by asking them how they made sense of the mixed message. Usually people pay more attention to the nonverbal cues than to the words. For example, a person may say, "I'm not upset with you." If the person's body language conveys discomfort or anger, however, you are likely to conclude that the person is, in fact, upset despite his or her words.

■ Dr. Albert Mehrabian, a professor at the University of California, Los Angeles, coined the term "body language." Working in the 1970s studying face-to-face, interpersonal communications he reported that his research showed that communication of feelings and attitudes goes beyond words. In response to the question "Which of the three is most likely to indicate the true feelings of someone?" Dr. Mehrabian's study subjects responded:

– Verbal: 7 percent

– Vocal: 38 percent

– Visual: 55 percent.

Ticket to Talk

Time: Basic Activity: 15–20   **Expanded Activity** ⊖: 25-30

Equipment: None

Materials: Index cards for ½ of the participants with the words "Ticket to Talk" printed on each

Handouts: None

Objectives:

- To reinforce the importance and impact of attentive listening
- To practice the skill of active listening

Procedure:

1. Organize the participants into pairs and give one person in each pair one "ticket-to-talk" card.
2. Ask the person with the card to tell his or her partner a short story, describe an experience, or give an opinion on any specific topic. Explain that the partners will have 2 minutes, and that you will let them know when the time is up.
3. Instruct the listeners to pay careful attention because at the conclusion of the 2 minutes, they will restate what their partner said using their own words. They must include all the points that they think are important to their partner.
4. Let participants know when 2 minutes have elapsed.
5. Give the participants the next set of instructions, as follows:
   - Listeners will say back what they heard from their partners in the first 2 minutes. Speakers will let their partners know if they got it right. In other words, did their partners really understand the important parts of what was said? Were there any omissions or misunderstandings?
   - In each pair, if the listener missed information or misunderstood some aspect, the speaker will restate and clarify that information.
   - The listeners will again say back what they heard until the speaker agrees that the listener fully understood the story. Partners will have up to 4 minutes to complete these steps of giving feedback and restating the story.
   - Once the listeners have successfully restated the story—or at the end of the 4-minute time period, the speakers will hand the listeners the ticket to talk.
6. Have the partners repeat the sequence. The listeners from the first round are the speakers in the second round. The new speakers will have to time themselves during the next round.
7. ⊖ When the partners have finished giving feedback and verifying that that the listener understood the speaker accurately in the second round, ask them to talk with each other about what happened in their pair. Once all the pairs have finished, reconvene the large group for the debriefing questions.

Debriefing Questions:

1. What was it like to do this activity?
2. What was easy?
3. What was difficult?
4. How does this activity relate to working effectively with diversity?
5. What can you take away from this activity?
6. How might it be helpful to you in your professional and personal life?

Ticket to Talk **Continued**

7. When you were the speaker, what behaviors indicated to you that your partner was really listening to you?

8. What was it like to be listened to and to hear your words said back?

9. When you were the listener, what helped you really hear your partner?

10. What could the speaker have done to help you?

11. What external factors can challenge our ability to listen to others fully?

12. What factors can get in the way internally?

13. How did you deal with those external and internal challenges in this activity?

14. How might you deal with them in everyday life?

Key Points:

■ Listening effectively is not easy. It requires full attention and concentration

■ When we are listening, it is important that we pay attention to the words and to the meanings and messages behind the words. For example, what nonverbal cues are coming across from the speaker? Are they congruent with the speaker's words or not? Effective listening involves using more senses than just your hearing.

■ Communication happens all the time. Even the way we listen communicates information to the person who is speaking. For example, through nonverbal cues, we can communicate how important we think the speaker is, an opinion about what is being said, and even whether we want to take the time to be listening. Behaviors that communicate such information include multitasking, looking around, checking a watch, nodding the head, leaning forward, tapping the foot, and so on.

■ Learning to manage our internal distracters is important to effective listening. This means letting go of our internal chatter or "self-talk." When we have a lot of internal chatter, it can actually be quite difficult to actually hear what someone else is really saying. We can misunderstand both verbal information and nonverbal cues.

What's on Your Mind?

Time: Basic Activity: 10–15 minutes   **Expanded Activity** e: 20–30 minutes

Equipment: None

Materials: Prepared Instruction Slips Labeled "A" and "B" (See Trainer's Notes)

Handouts: None

Objectives:

■ To show the impact of behavior on the communication process
■ To explore the impact of positive communication on relationships

Procedure:

1. Organize the participants into pairs. Give each pair one "A" slip and one "B" slip. (See Trainer's Notes.)
2. Ask the pairs to discuss a social, entertainment, or sporting event while following the instructions on their slips. Allow 2 or 3 minutes.
3. Reconvene the large group and lead a discussion using the debriefing questions below.

Debriefing Questions:

1. How did that go? What did you notice during the activity?
2. If you had a "B" slip, what did you observe about your partner's behavior and words? What was the effect it had on you? What thoughts and feelings did you notice?
3. If you had an "A" slip, what did you observe about your partner's behavior and words? What was the effect it had on you? What thoughts and feelings did you notice?
4. Everyone, how did these thoughts and feelings affect your engagement in the discussion?
5. How do you build rapport with others? What connections do you see between this activity and your day-to-day life?
6. What can you take away from this activity?
e 7. If you had a "B" slip, what was it like giving negative messages to your partner?
e 8. If you had an "A" slip, what was it like receiving negative messages from your partner?
e 9. If you had an "A" slip, what was it like giving positive messages to your partner?
e 10. If you had a "B" slip, what was it like receiving consistently positive messages from your partner?
e 11. Have you experienced this pattern of communication in the workplace? At home? What have been the outcomes?
e 12. Which communication styles are most challenging for you? Why?
e 13. How do you respond in those situations? What is helpful?

Key Points:

■ Interacting with people with a negative view makes communication and teamwork more challenging.
■ Working with people who are habitually negative often reduces our willingness to communicate or collaborate with them. This can start a negative communication cycle.
■ It is important to remember how much our attitude and mood affects the people around us. Working in a diverse environment can be a challenge, and it helps when people put their best foot forward.

What's on Your Mind? Continued

- Positive communication habits build rapport and create a constructive working environment in which people focus their energy and focus on solving problems and attaining goals.
- Dealing with someone who is habitually negative demands that we actively work with ourselves to not start or strengthen a negative communication cycle.

Trainer's Notes:

- For each pair of partners, prepare or copy two instruction slips of paper, labeled "A" and "B," with the following instructions:

Instruction Slip A
■ Tell your partner only positive and friendly things about the topic.
■ Say good things about the person you are talking with.
■ Don't talk about yourself.
Instruction Slip B
■ Be as negative as possible. For example, complain about everything.
■ Brag about yourself.
■ Take over as much of the conversation as you can.

I Can't See for Looking

Time: Basic Activity: 15 minutes   **Expanded Activity** ⓔ: 30 minutes

Equipment: None

Materials: Pairs of Prepared Instruction Slips, labeled "A" and "B" and "C" and "D" (See Trainer's Notes)

ⓔ **Handout:** I Can't See for Looking—Comparing Communication Norms and Values from Different Cultures

Objectives:

- To increase awareness of the influence of culture on communication
- To increase awareness of the challenges involved in changing one's style of communication to be effective in situations where the norms and expected behaviors are unfamiliar

Procedure:

1. Give each participant one instruction slip. Tell the participants to keep their instructions confidential.
2. Ask the participants to find a partner—preferably someone in the room that they don't know well.
3. Direct the newly formed pairs to ask questions in order to discover at least two things they did not know about their partner while following the instructions on their slip. Allow 2 minutes.
4. Reconvene the large group and conduct a debriefing on the basic activity using debriefing questions 1 through 6 below. If you are using the expanded version of the activity, return to step 5 after asking debriefing questions 1 through 5. ⓔ Divide the large group into small groups of four to six people.
ⓔ 5. Distribute the handout titled "Comparing Communication Cultural Norms and Values."
ⓔ 6. Ask the participants to review and discuss the information on the handout with their group. Ask them to focus their discussion on the following areas:
   - How do you approach the situations and elements listed?
   - In what ways is your approach congruent with mainstream U.S. culture?
   - In what ways does your approach differ from mainstream U.S. culture? What has influenced you in those areas?
7. After 10 minutes, reconvene the full group.
8. Ask a person to act as reporter for the group with Instruction Slip A. Have that person read what was written on their slip of paper. Do the same with the groups that had Instruction Slips B, C, and D. As the reporters read their instructions, record the following elements of culture on a flipchart labeled "Elements of Culture":
   - Eye contact
   - Emotion expressed
   - Distance and gestures
   - Volume and pacing
   - Initiating and responsiveness
   - Topics of conversation
9. Explain that in the exercise the participants were able to directly experience elements of culture colliding in communication.

I Can't See for Looking **Continued**

Debriefing Questions:

1. What words describe your first reactions to your instructions?

2. What thoughts and feelings did you notice as you were interacting with your partner? (Record the participants' answers on a flipchart labeled "Thoughts and Feelings.")

3. What behaviors from your partner did you find disrespectful, annoying, or embarrassing? What made those behaviors uncomfortable for you?

4. Look back at your exchange. What assumptions or questions about your partner came up in your mind as you were interacting? (For example, in the case of a partner who looked away, you may have assumed that the partner was hiding something, was bored, or was habitually disrespectful.)

5. How does your experience of this activity relate to everyday life?

6. How does this activity relate to communication, diversity, and inclusion?

7. How will this experience help you be more effective when communicating with others in the workplace? What else did you learn that you can apply at work? (Note: If you are using the Expanded Activity, this question should only be used to close the activity.)

ⓔ 8. What did you discuss with your team?

ⓔ 9. What did you learn about other cultures?

ⓔ Key Points:

- Communication with culturally different co-workers can become difficult when we are unaware of differences in communication-related norms and values.

- When we are unaware of differences in culture, we are likely to make assumptions about a person who communicates or behaves differently based on our own cultural norms.

- Learning to communicate according to norms that are different from the ones we were brought up to value takes us out of our comfort zone. It makes it more challenging to get our message across to others because we don't know how to interpret the feedback that comes to us from listeners. We feel like a fish out of water, so the whole interaction can be uncomfortable and difficult to manage.

- ⓔ When communicating across cultures, messages can become distorted because of misperceptions and misinterpretations of words, tone of voice, and body language. The more we learn about cross-cultural communication, the more we are open to others. This open attitude often encourages communication—even in circumstances that are difficult.

- ⓔ If you deal frequently with people from a specific culture, it can be very helpful to make a point of learning about that culture in order to be more effective in communicating and working with colleagues or customers.

I Can't See for Looking **Continued**

Trainer's Notes:

Copy instruction slips A, B, C, and D and cut out the strips. Make enough to give each participant one strip. Distribute the sets of instructions as evenly as possible. Make sure that some pairs of participants receive the combination of A and B instructions and that other pairs receive the combination of C and D instructions.

Instruction Slip A

■ Avoid eye contact when speaking to your partner.

■ Do not show any emotion or react to your partner when he or she is speaking.

Instruction Slip B

■ Stand about 6 inches closer to your partner than you normally would.

■ Use gestures often when you are speaking.

Instruction Slip C

■ Speak more loudly than you normally would and interrupt your partner fairly frequently.

■ Initiate conversation by asking a lot of questions (including personal ones).

Instruction Slip D

■ Speak more softly than you normally would and avoid interrupting your partner.

■ Silently count to six before responding, and don't initiate conversation or ask questions.

I Can't See for Looking ⊝ Handout

Comparing Communication Norms and Values from Different Cultures

This comparison of cultural norms can help you identify and understand ways in which cultural norms and values influence communication related behavior. This kind of information can help to interrupt judgments about a person that are based on stereotypes rather than real understanding of the person.

Aspect of Culture	Mainstream U.S. Culture	Other Cultures
Sense of self and space	Informal Handshake	Formal Hugs, bows, handshakes
Communication and language	Explicit, direct communication Emphasis on content—meaning found in words	Implicit, indirect communication Emphasis on context—meaning found around words
Eye contact	Moderate to very direct	Minimal Moderate Very Direct
Physical proximity	18 inches to 3 feet	3 feet or more 0–18 inches
Voice volume	Louder than average	Soft spoken Louder than average
Interrupting others	Comfortable	Extremely rude Comfortable
Hand gestures	Comfortable	Pointing is considered poor etiquette Beckoning is very offensive OK (thumbs up) and "V" for victory signs have sexual connotations
Physical (nonsexual) touching	Uncomfortable	Comfortable Uncomfortable Varied

Chapter 9
Diversity Issues

Everybody can be great...because anybody can serve.
You don't have to have a college degree to serve.
You don't have to make your subject and verb agree to serve.
You only need a heart full of grace. A soul generated by love.
MARTIN LUTHER KING, JR.

Our awareness of diversity has gone through quantum growth over the last 20 years. Although issues related to race and gender remain important, others that have always been present have emerged for discussion and need to be addressed to create inclusive organizations and communities. These include issues regarding religion, sexual orientation, physical ability, mental illness, age, language, health, parenting, and caring for aging parents.

Learning about each of these issues is a process, not a one-time event. In your sessions, you will discover that participants bring different levels of awareness and knowledge about diversity topics depending on their life. When people begin to learn about any new topic, they often bring an attitude that can be called "unconscious unawareness." This attitude also has been nicknamed "clueless." Basically, what it comes down to is that we don't know what we don't know. We usually are comfortable at this stage of the game because we think we are knowledgeable when in reality we have a big blind spot.

As learning continues, the next attitude that emerges is "conscious unawareness." This attitude differs from the earlier one because we are no longer comfortable. Most people experience conscious unawareness as an uncomfortable, "heads-up" moment. This is the moment when we realize that a group of people consistently experiences difficulties in ways that we had absolutely no awareness of. The next attitude that emerges is "conscious awareness." At this stage we usually feel awkward and out of our comfort zone. We are seeking to understand the experiences of others and want to know what we can do to communicate respect and support. Often we also are trying out new behaviors and roles to be effective in valuing diversity and strengthening inclusion.

The final attitude is that of "unconscious awareness." At this stage the learning we were doing in the previous stages has been mastered and we automatically practice effective behaviors. We are back in our comfort zone and feeling good—until something comes our way to make us realize that we are unconsciously unaware about a new topic or situation.

The good news is that we can choose to continue to learn and that with practice and attention we improve both our understanding and our skills. The bad news is that learning is likely to be continuous—a fact that is as true for diversity facilitators as it is for workshop participants.

This section presents activities that you can use to explore specific topics of diversity and ways of addressing them effectively. We have not included activities for all possible topics. The activities can, however, be adapted to different diversity topics as needed.

Getting Out of the Fishbowl

Time: Basic Activity: 15–20 minutes   **Expanded Activity** [e]: 30–40 minutes

Equipment: Flipchart

Materials: Flipchart and art supplies (crayons and paper or modeling clay or play dough in a variety of colors)

Handout: Getting out of the Fishbowl

Objective:

■ To define and clarify the meanings of the terms *diversity*, *culture*, and *inclusion*

Procedure:

1. Organize participants into three groups of up to five people. If you have more than 15 people in your session, assign the terms to more than one group as needed.
2. Introduce the activity by saying "A visitor from another planet is coming to see us at the end of this activity. This visitor does understand English, though there are some words in our language that do not translate into the language of that planet. To help our visitor understand what we are talking about in this session, we will offer clear definitions of three words that come up a lot in discussions and dialogues related to diversity: *culture*, *diversity*, and *inclusion*. Coming up with these definitions will be your task during this activity.
3. Distribute the handout titled "Getting Out of the Fishbowl." Assign each word to one or more groups. Tell them this is the word they will define for this activity.
4. Review the instructions on the handout with participants.
[e] 5. Instruct each group to draw a picture or use any of the materials provided to represent the meaning of their word.
[e] 6. Allow 15 minutes.
[e] 7. Ask the groups to post their pictures (or place their objects) around the room.
[e] 8. Invite the participants to stretch their legs and take a walk around the art gallery.
9. Reconvene the full group for presentations.
10. Ask each reporter to present the definition the group came up with. Ask the participants to listen carefully to the definitions provided by each of the other groups to be sure they understand the thinking of the other groups.
11. After all the definitions have been heard, ask each reporter to present his or her group's response to the second question on the handout.

Debriefing Questions:

1. What was it like to do this activity?
2. What were some of the challenges you faced as a group?
3. How did you resolve differences of opinion?
4. What did you discover about these words and their meanings?
[e] 5. What was it like to create a nonverbal representation of your assigned word?
[e] 6. What discussions (if any) took place during that part of the activity?

Getting Out of the Fishbowl Continued

Key Points:

- *Culture*, *diversity*, and *inclusion* are key words in any conversation about diversity.
- It is easy for us to use the words and assume that we share the same definitions when in fact they often mean different things to different people.
- Putting words into pictures carries three primary benefits. First, it helps clarify meaning and allows new connections or ideas to emerge. Second, it is a fun way for a group to work together to examine a word or a concept. Third, it creates a product that can be displayed or photographed and distributed as a reminder of the group's collaboration.
- We have settled on some definitions for each of these words and have found it helpful to make them explicit in our work. In summary, an easy way of understanding each of these words and how they relate to each other is to keep three main points in mind: First, diversity is all the ways people and things are different. Second, culture is the way we behave and act differently. Third, inclusiveness encompasses and embraces both diversity and cultural differences.

Trainer's Notes:

- Through the exercise, the participants will arrive at their own definitions of the terms *culture*, *diversity*, and *inclusion*. During the reports and debriefing, emphasize points as necessary to ensure that the participants' understanding of these terms is consistent with the following definitions
- One of the best definitions of the term *culture* appears in the *Concise Columbia Encyclopedia* (Houghton Mifflin Company, 1995): "Culture is the way of life of a given society, passed down from one generation to the next through learning and experience." Culture is many-layered and complex. Its components include patterns of values, beliefs, communication, language, definitions of family, gender roles, personal space, status, traditions, holidays, and more. Our cultural identities form as we experience membership in groups or societies including ethnicity, nationality, family lineage, sexual orientation, religion, sports, special interest, profession, employer, disability, age, and gender just to mention a few.
- The term *diversity* can be defined as the collection of similarities and differences we carry with us at all times, based on the characteristics we were born with, the experiences we have had, and the choices we have made. The term *inclusion* can be defined as the process of ensuring that people feel included and valued in an organization or a community. In an inclusive organization, each person's resources and contributions are recognized, respected, and used in service to the organization's goals; it is a place where people feel valued, respected, and heard, and where people are fully able to contribute. (Adapted from Richard A. Friend, Richard Friend & Associates, Inc., 2002.)

Getting Out of the Fishbowl **Handout**

Getting Out of the Fishbowl

1. You have been assigned the task of creating a definition of one of the following words:

   ■ Culture
   ■ Inclusion
   ■ Diversity

   Prepare to present your definition on a flipchart.

2. Prepare to talk about the relationship between your assigned word and the other two words that have been assigned to other groups.

3. Designate a reporter to present your group's ideas to the full group.

4. You have 15 minutes.

Vision of Diversity and Inclusion

Time: Basic Activity: 15–20 minutes   **Expanded Activity : 30–40 minutes

Equipment: Flipchart

Materials: Paper and crayons

Handouts: None

Objectives:

- To give participants an opportunity to clarify what an inclusive environment that values diversity would look like and what it would feel like being there
- To explore what it means to be a diversity leader

Procedure:

1. Distribute paper and crayons to all participants.
2. Tell the participants to take a few minutes to consider what an inclusive environment that values diversity would look like and how it would feel being in such a place.
3. Ask them to take a crayon and describe what came to their mind without using words. Explain that artistic excellence is not the focus—there will be no critique of talent or skill. Allow 5 minutes.
4. Ask the participants to include themselves in the picture as a person who helps to make their vision come true.
5. Put the participants into groups of three or four people. Ask them to share their pictures with their colleagues and explain what is behind the images they used. Remind the participants that this is not a time to critique art but rather a time to explore ideas and visions. Allow 10 minutes.
6. Reconvene the group.

Debriefing Questions:

1. What was it like to put your vision on paper without words?
2. What themes emerged in your small-group discussions?
3. How did it feel to talk about your vision?
4. Why is it important to have a personal vision about diversity and inclusion?
5. Why is it valuable to have a common vision about diversity and inclusion among team members or within an organization?
6. What makes it challenging to consistently behave in ways that value diversity and promote inclusion?
7. How do you deal with those obstacles?
8. What sources of inspiration are helpful? How do other people inspire you? Who inspires you?
9. What was it like to put yourself in the picture as a diversity leader?
10. What external obstacles get in the way of contributing to your vision?
11. What internal obstacles can get in the way of contributing to your vision?
12. What can we do to be more effective as diversity leaders?
13. How do we influence others? The person we report to? Peers? Direct reports? Co-workers in other departments or on other teams? External customers?
14. How does this activity relate to your day-to-day life?

Vision of Diversity and Inclusion **Continued**

Key Points:

■ Inspiration and vision are important drivers for any change. They are important for individuals, for teams, and for organizations.

■ A common vision helps groups of people work efficiently toward a goal.

■ Once we have identified a vision or a goal, obstacles always arise. It is helpful to have a plan to address those obstacles. It is also important to pay attention to what inspires us *not* to get stopped by those obstacles.

 ■ Leadership is often thought to be "somebody else's job." In organizational life, supervisors, managers, and executives are formal leaders; however, everyone is an informal leader. Each person's actions and words contribute to making the vision of inclusion become real—or not.

■ It is important to not let external obstacles get in the way of doing what we can. Sometimes we can do more to influence a situation than we think at first. It is often worth a second look.

Trainer's Notes:

■ Demonstrate equal appreciation for all the images presented by participants. The most important part of the activity is the process of creating it and the discussion afterwards, not the end product.

■ This activity encourages people to step up to the plate as formal or informal leaders. Some participants may resist the idea. It is important to make clear that it is of benefit to each of us to see how we can expand our influence and do what is in our control in service to our vision. This is not about holding people responsible for things they can't do anything about. Rather, it is about encouraging people to find steps they can take to influence the people and the environment around them.

Diversity Groundhog

Time: Basic Activity: 20–30 minutes   **Expanded Activity:** 50–60 minutes

Equipment: Two flipcharts

Materials: None

Handouts:

- ■ Handout #1: Diversity Groundhog
- e ■ Handout #2: Diversity Scorecard

Objectives:

- ■ To identify an organization's current approach and response to diversity and inclusion
- ■ To identify possible steps that organization and its members or employees can take to leverage diversity and inclusion for the mutual benefit and gain of everyone
- e ■ To consider ways in which the participant's organization may or may not be responding effectively to diversity or strengthening inclusion

Procedure:

1. Divide the participants into groups of three or four people, with each group selecting a reporter. Designate half of the groups as "Warning Shadow" groups and the other half as "No Shadow" groups. Give all participants a copy of the handout titled "Diversity Groundhog" and ask them to read it.

2. Ask the Warning Shadow groups to discuss how management and individuals might deal with the denial response. Tell the No Shadow groups to discuss the same questions with respect to the loose-cannon behavior. To encourage discussion, you can pose the following additional questions:
   - ■ What are some of the issues that need to be addressed by the organization?
   - ■ What issues might individuals be facing?
   - ■ Why might people respond to the situation they way they do (denial response or loose cannon)?

3. Direct each group to record its responses to the questions on a flipchart, and designate a person who will report out to the large group. Allow 10 minutes.

4. On reconvening the large group, ask for the groups' reports and have the participants examine and compare the small groups' responses. Comparing the lists they have generated, what similarities do they see? What differences?

e 5. Pass out the handout titled "Diversity Scorecard" and allow participants to complete it individually. Ask them to rate their organization's record in valuing diversity and creating inclusion.

e 6. Working in the same small groups, ask participants to discuss and compare their answers with each other. Tell them to give examples of actions that support the ratings they gave. Direct them to select a different reporter to present the themes of discussion.

Debriefing Questions:

1. What connections do you make between the lists you generated and what you see happening in your organization?

e 2. With regard to the Diversity Scorecard, what did you discuss in your groups?

e 3. What are some examples of actions that earned an SE rating from the perspective of employees or internal customers? What actions earned an ME rating? An NME rating?

Diversity Groundhog **Continued**

[e] 4. What are some examples of actions that earned an SE rating from the perspective of external customers? An ME rating? An NME rating?

[e] 5. What can be done to consistently earn an SE rating from employees or internal customers? External customers?

6. What can you take away from this activity?

Key Points:

■ Diversity is a reality. It's not coming, it's here.

■ Companies and individuals that acknowledge and leverage diversity increase their opportunities to be successful.

■ Companies and individuals that do not acknowledge and leverage diversity may hinder their long-term success because managing diversity is a key teamwork and leadership competency.

Trainer's Notes:

■ Focus the participants' discussion on the advantages and benefits of dealing with diversity as well as the barriers to acknowledging and leveraging diversity.

■ An optional way to conduct this activity is to divide the participants into teams to come up with recommendations for each of the identified challenges and have them report out their suggestions. Or you may have the participants shout out suggestions as you record them on a flipchart.

■ Ask the group, "As an individual, what can you do to demonstrate that you value diversity and inclusion in the workplace?"

Diversity Groundhog Handout

Diversity Groundhog Story

There is a mythical creature called the Diversity Groundhog. On February 2 each year, this creature emerges from its burrow, where it has been hibernating for the winter, only to discover that extensive changes have occurred in the company. The demographics of the employee base have shifted and now include more people of color, immigrants, and women. Changes among other stakeholders also are evident, including the community, board members, suppliers, and end-users of products and services. Some culture clashes have occurred. Still, top management seems unwilling to pay attention to those changes and their effects on the company.

The Diversity Groundhog will exhibit one of two possible reactions:

1. If the Diversity Groundhog has spotted a progressive and bothersome Warning Shadow, it hastily retreats back into its burrow to emerge again sometime in the future, leaving matters unresolved. When this happens, the company—like the Diversity Groundhog—is in denial, burying itself and hiding from its diversity issues, which eventually will likely come back to haunt it.

2. If the diversity events suddenly appeared, neither anticipated nor acknowledged, the Diversity Groundhog will have seen no Warning Shadow. In this case, the Diversity Groundhog stays outside its burrow and behaves like a loose cannon. The Diversity Groundhog will not hibernate again, and the situation must be dealt with immediately.

Diversity Groundhog e **Handout**

Diversity Scorecard Rating System

SE As a company, they rate us as *surpassing their expectations* (SE). Their experience is that we are proactive in our approach to diversity and inclusion. They see us as diversity and inclusion leaders.

ME They rate us as *meeting their expectations* (ME). Their experience is that most of the time we react positively to resolve issues of diversity and inclusion.

NME They rate us as *not meeting their expectations* (NME). Their experience is that we do not value diversity and inclusion, no matter what our words or policies may be. They do not experience us as "walking the talk"; rather, they see us as resistant to change with regard to diversity issues.

Diversity Scorecard

	Ratings			
Our Internal and External Customers	**SE**	**ME**	**NME**	**Actions that Promote an SE Rating**
1. Our non-management employees (internal customers) feel valued, respected, and heard.				
2. Our managerial employees (internal customers) feel valued, respected, and heard.				
3. Our vendors and suppliers (external customers) feel valued, respected, and heard.				
4. Our community and product or service end-users (external customers) feel valued, respected, and heard.				
5. Our shareholders (external customers) feel valued, respected, and heard.				
6. Our board (external customers) feels valued, respected, and heard.				

Win a Few, Lose a Few!

Time: Basic Activity: 45–60 minutes

Equipment: Flipchart

Materials: None

Handouts:

- Handout #1: Rules for Win A Few, Lose A Few (Team 1 version has ***no special instructions***)
- Handout #2: Rules for Win A Few, Lose A Few (Team 2 version has ***special instructions***)

Objectives:

- To illustrate that rules often are applied selectively
- To offer an experience demonstrating how it feels to exclude and be excluded by others

Procedure:

1. Divide the participants into two teams.
2. Give the following explanation to both teams simultaneously:
   "We are going to play a game with five rounds. We will give you written rules to follow while playing. A different member of each team will have to answer one question in each round, and scores based on correct answers will be recorded on the flipchart. The winning team is the team with the most points at the end of the game."
3. Take Team #1 into the hall or another room and distribute Handout #1 (***without*** special instructions), Rules for Win a Few, Lose a Few! Ask the team members to remain where they are until the other team has received its rules.
4. Return to Team #2 and distribute Handout #2 (***with*** special instructions), Rules For Win a Few, Lose a Few! Point out to Team #2 that they have the answers but Team #1 does not. Review the rules and instruct the members of Team #2 to determine a strategy to ensure that Team #1 does not discover that they have the answers.
5. Bring Team #1 back into the room and instruct each team to stand in a line on opposite sides of the room.
6. Using the list of questions and answers in the Trainer's Notes, begin the game by asking Team #1 the first question. If the answer is correct, record one point on the flipchart for Team #1. If the answer is incorrect, record a score of zero.
7. Ask the next question of Team #2. If the answer is correct, record two points on the flipchart for Team #2. Ignore any comments from Team #1 about the difference in allotted points. If the answer is incorrect, record a score of zero for Team #2.
8. Continue going from team to team, asking a different player each time to respond to the next question. Note: Team #1 is asked the odd-numbered questions and Team #2 is asked the even-numbered questions.
9. At the end of the game, have the participants return to their seats.

Debriefing Questions:

1. Beginning with Team #1, ask the following questions:
   - What do you think has been going on this game?
   - How did you feel about the way you were treated?
   - When did you notice that the rules were different?
   - How did you respond? Why did you continue to play? Did your desire to win increase or decrease during the game?

Win a Few, Lose a Few! Continued

2. Ask Team #2 the following questions:
   - How did it feel being a member of your team?
   - How did you feel about the way Team #1 was treated?
   - How far were you willing to go in playing the game?
   - What did your behavior tell you about yourself? About the other members of your team?
3. Ask the following questions of the whole group:
   - At work, are the rules the same for everybody?
   - What can happen in the workplace when people feel that rules do not apply equally to everyone?
   - What can you do if you feel that you, or any group, are being treated differently from others in the organization? Are some people being excluded?

Key Points:

- Excluding others takes energy and effort.
- When we are excluded, we are not able to deliver 100 percent of our capabilities because we are distracted by self-doubt and self-questioning. In addition, we usually deploy some active or passive strategy to defend or protect ourselves from uncomfortable feelings such as hurt, anger, and vulnerability. All of this activity takes energy, which then isn't available for work.
- Inclusion increases the amount of energy available for individual and organizational creativity and success. Exclusion is a barrier to both creativity and productivity.

Trainer's Notes:

- It is best to have an experienced diversity facilitator—or at least an experienced facilitator—conduct this game.
- This game can be part of a total diversity workshop. It also can stand alone as an icebreaker for a focus group.
- To prepare the flipchart before the game begins, draw a line down the center of the page and, at the top, label one side "Team #1" and the other side "Team #2."
- Prepare yourself by carefully reviewing the two rule sheets used in this game. Remember that they are different. The rule sheets should be handed out only when the teams are in separate locations.
- Keep the game moving and do not answer challenges by either team. When Team #1 answers a question incorrectly, make disparaging remarks, such as "That figures." "I didn't think you would know the answer." "Where did these people come from?" or "It looks like they don't know very much."
- Give Team #2 lots of encouragement and praise them when they answer questions correctly.

Win a Few, Lose a Few Q & A Key

1. According to the U.S. Census Bureau, over the past 5 years seven states absorbed the most immigrants. Name five of those states.

   Answer: Arizona, California, Florida, Illinois, New Jersey, New York, and Texas

2. Give the title of the diversity book by Roosevelt Thomas.

   Answer: Beyond Race & Gender: Unleashing the Power of Your Total Work Force by Managing Diversity

3. What was the name of the Shoshone Indian woman who helped guide the Lewis and Clark Expedition in 1804–1806?

   Answer: Sacagawea

4. What is the comfortable distance you should stand from a person, according to U.S. mainstream communication style?

   Answer: An arm's length, or 36"

5. What is the West Coast equivalent to Ellis Island?

   Answer: Angel Island, in northern California

6. In American culture, it is considered appropriate to maintain eye contact for 1 second and then to look away. True or False?

   Answer: True

7. The term Generation X refers to people born between which years?

   Answer: 1961–1980

8. What state has the only royal palace in the United States?

   Answer: Hawaii–the Iolani Palace

9. In what year was the Americans with Disabilities Act passed?

   Answer: 1990

10. In what year was The Vietnam Era Veterans Readjustment Act passed?

    Answer: 1974

Win a Few, Lose a Few! Handout #1

Rules for Win a Few, Lose a Few!

1. Your task is to select five team members who will score the points for your team by answering questions posed by the facilitator.

2. Each of those five people will answer one question. Each correct answer earns your team one point.

3. You are allowed only one answer. If it's incorrect, you do not get a second chance, and receive 0 points for that round.

4. The people designated to answer questions may *not* check with their teammates for help on their questions. They must answer individually. You are not allowed to applaud your team.

Win a Few, Lose a Few! Handout #2

Rules for Win a Few, Lose a Few!

Special Instructions

Do not share your rules or show any emotion as you look over them because we have also provided you with the answers.

1. Your task is to select five team members who will score the points for your team by answering questions posed by the facilitator.

2. Each of those five people will answer one question. Each correct answer earns your team two points.

3. Applaud your team after your points are recorded on the flipchart.

Below you will find the answers to the questions. ***Do not let the other team know that you have the answers.***

1. CA, TX, NY, FL, IL, NJ, and AZ
2. *Beyond Race & Gender: Unleashing the Power of Your Total Work Force by Managing Diversity*
3. Sacagawea
4. An arm's length, or 36"
5. Angel Island, in northern California
6. True
7. 1961–1980
8. Hawaii–the Iolani Palace
9. 1990
10. 1974

If I Were in Your Shoes

Time: Basic Activity: 15–20 minutes   **Expanded Activity** e: 20–30 minutes

Equipment: A separate breakout room set up as an obstacle course.

Materials: Blindfolds for each participant (*Optional:* Use inexpensive large handkerchiefs, bandanas, or scarves, so participants can keep them and you avoid washing and disinfecting blindfolds for re-use.)

Handout: Obstacle Course Debriefing Questionnaire

Objectives:

- To give participants an opportunity to experience what it might be like to be vision impaired
- To give participants practice at clear and concise communication

Procedure:

1. Before beginning the activity, set up the obstacle course. Place masking tape on the floor to outline the course. Obstacles should include things that cannot hurt or in any way injure participants, such as plastic spoons, foam cups, plastic garbage cans, conference table chairs, and so forth. Place the obstacles strategically on the course so participants have to wind their way around and between obstacles. The participants will work in pairs, and the entire course should take no more than 10 minutes for each couple to navigate.

2. Begin the activity by giving a blindfold to each participant. Say, "Your goal is to work with a blindfolded partner to navigate that person through an obstacle course without touching any obstacles. You may give verbal instructions only."

3. Direct the participants to pair up with another participant and decide who will be the blindfolded walker and who will be the coach in the first round. Tell the participants that they will switch roles for the second round.

4. Tell the participants who will be blindfolded to put on their blindfolds. Direct the coaches to navigate with their partners from the training room to the obstacle-course room, line up with their partners outside the obstacle-course, and wait for the next instruction.

5. Once the participants have lined up outside the obstacle-course room, let them know that both coach and blindfolded walker will be in the room at the same time; however, only the blindfolded walker will set foot inside the course. Coaches will give verbal instructions from the sidelines and may not touch their partner at any time. Direct the pairs to plan their communication strategy. Allow 3 minutes.

6. Take pairs inside the obstacle course room. Instruct coaches to start their partners through the obstacle course. Their task is to ensure that their blindfolded partners do not touch any obstacles.

7. When each blindfolded partner has completed the course, direct the partners to switch roles and navigate the course for the second time.

8. For each pair, when the course has been completed for the second time, direct the coach to take the blindfolded partner back to the training room.

e 9. When all pairs have return to the training room, distribute the Obstacle Course Debriefing Questionnaire. Have the participants discuss the questions with their partners. Give them 7 minutes.

Debriefing Questions:

1. What did you learn about what it might be like to be visually impaired?
2. What helped you build trust with your partner? What eroded trust?

If I Were in Your Shoes **Continued**

3. What can you take away from this activity related to diversity, inclusion, and communication in the workplace? (Note: If you are using the Expanded Activity, this question should only be used to close the activity.)

4. What experiences have you had working with people who have a physical disability?

5. What did you learn in such situations? What were the challenges? What were the benefits?

6. If you have not had any such experiences, how might your lack of experience with this issue affect your working relationships or expectations?

7. What assumptions or stereotypes are you aware of with respect to working with people with disabilities?

Key Points:

- We'll never know, fully, what it's like to be blind unless we become blind. This exercise, however, can offer some insight into the challenges faced by people with visual impairments in the workplace.

- Consciously or unconsciously, people who are sighted rely on their eyes to pick up nonverbal messages as well as a means of communication. When one party does not have sight, words and tone of voice become more important elements in communication.

- In this activity you also got a chance to experience the impact of effective communication in building or eroding trust and confidence.

Trainer's Notes:

- Obstacles can include paper cups, pieces of rope, paper plates, balls large enough to avoid tripping or twisted ankles. Other toys also work well. Some people make this a three-dimensional obstacle course by hanging things from the ceiling or stretching masking tape across the room from wall to wall. Clearly mark the beginning and the end of the course with masking tape or a piece of rope.

- You may allow three or four couples to navigate the obstacle course at once. Manage entrances and exits into the room to avoid a backup. Stay in the obstacle-course room once the first pair enters until the last pair leaves. Remember to remove all tape and obstacles and return the room to its original setup before the end of the day.

If I Were in Your Shoes **Handout**

Obstacle Course Debriefing Questionnaire

Continuing to work in with your obstacle course partner, discuss and answer the following questions about that experience. Be prepared to discuss your observations with the larger group.

1. How well did your strategy for communicating inside the obstacle course work? Did you need to make any changes in your agreed-upon strategy? If so, what were they?

2. How did both of you react if the walker hit an obstacle?

3. Which role was more comfortable for you: blindfolded walker or coach? Why?

4. What did you learn about yourself?

5. What increased or eroded trust?

6. Have you ever worked with a person with a physical disability or do you know someone with a disability? Tell the story. What did you learn from this person?

Chapter 10
Conflict Resolution

As long as the differences and diversities of mankind exist, democracy must allow for compromise, for accommodation, and for the recognition of differences.

EUGENE MCCARTHY

Whenever two or more people interact over time, there will be conflict. It is inevitable. Sources of conflict vary. They include differences of opinion, personality, desired outcomes, expectations, hopes, life experience, and culture.

Culture can be a factor in conflict in many ways, from misinterpretation of behavior to ways in which people approach conflict. It can also make situations where differences in personality or desired outcomes are the primary issues more difficult to resolve.

Culture-related misunderstandings appear in many forms. This fact is important to understand because we frequently discount the effects of culture on conflict situations. For example, some conflicts may be caused by or aggravated by limited language skills, accents, differences in customs for personal hygiene, or even differences in appearance, such as dress or physical characteristics. Other conflicts may arise because of assumptions, perceptions, and values that are based in culture.

To deal constructively with any conflict, it is important to learn about the point of view and experience of the other person as well as to understand our own perspective. It is also important to understand that we each have our own personal habits for how we deal with conflict. Some of these habits are less effective than others.

Many of us are still learning how to deal effectively with conflicts, and issues related to diversity may seem to make a difficult situation even harder. We can, however, learn and practice skills that help us better manage conflict or recovering a relationship after a conflict. Sometimes the best we can do doesn't work very well, but as we get to know others better and as we get to know ourselves, the awareness, insight, and appreciation that can help us resolve conflicts effectively come more easily. Accepting that we must continue to learn and develop our skills is a key to eventually resolving specific situations and improving our ability to deal with conflict in general.

How Far to Push?

Time: Basic Activity: 10–15 minutes   **Expanded Activity e:** 20–30 minutes

Equipment: Flipchart

Materials: None

Handouts: None

Objectives:

- To help participants identify the dynamics of reacting to a confrontation
- To increase participants' awareness of their own reactions when they are approached by someone who behaves as an adversary

Procedure:

1. Introduce the activity by explaining to the participants that they will work with a partner for a few minutes without words, instead using hand-to-hand contact. Direct them to stand up and find a partner who is about the same height.
2. Tell the participants that they will work with their partners palm to palm. Ask if any participants would prefer not to partici-pate. Note: People may not want to participate in this activity for various reasons, including health constraints, cultural con-straints, or personal preferences. If a participant indicates discomfort and no accommodation can be made, suggest that the participant observe the activity and prepare to report his or her observations during the debriefing.
3. Assist any participants who have not yet found partners so that the entire group is divided into pairs.
4. Ask the pairs to stand facing each other. Direct them to stand with their feet shoulder-width apart and flat on the floor. Direct them to place both palms against the palms of their partner. Ask them to decide who will be Partner A and who will be Part-ner B. Once that decision has been made, direct the As to try to push the Bs so that they move their feet. Allow about 1 minute, then direct participants to switch so that the Bs push the As with the goal of making them move their feet.
5. After 1 minute reconvene the large group.

Debriefing Questions:

1. What happened during this activity?
2. What happened when you were asked to push your partner? What was his or her initial response? What happened when you continued to push? Did that response change?
3. Did you ease up on your pushing? If yes, what happened?
4. Reflect back to your experience when you were being pushed. What was your response? How much time did it take for that response to occur?
5. What connections do you see between this activity and workplace situations?
6. What can you take away from this activity that will help you deal with resistance you encounter in the workplace?
7. **e** What influences how you respond to being pushed and demonstrating resistance? (A sample response might be "At work, there is no point in resisting, you just have to go along.")
8. **e** What is your greatest challenge in dealing with resistance from other people? What can you do to overcome that challenge and promote synergistic, win-win outcomes?
9. **e** What is your greatest challenge dealing with your own resistance? What helps you re-orient yourself once your automatic resistance has been triggered?

How Far to Push? **Continued**

Key Points:

- People respond in various ways to conflict and confrontation.
- People have different ways of dealing with resistance encountered at work and at home.
- The ways we deal with resistance are influenced by the norms of our culture, our individual styles, and the context of the conflict.
- Increasing trust helps to reduce resistance.
- Response to resistance often depends on culture as well as on former experiences with the situation and others involved.
- Dealing with resistance in others demands patience and steady effort to create a positive climate.

Double or Nothing

Time: Basic Activity: 15 minutes   **Expanded Activity** e : 25 minutes

Equipment: Prepared flipchart

Materials: Real one-dollar bills or phony money, such as Monopoly Game money or money created using clipart

Handouts: None

Objective:

■ To explore negotiating in relation to culture and values

Procedure:

1. At the beginning of the activity, give each participant a one-dollar bill or ask the participants to take out a one-dollar bill. Note: If you use real dollar bills, you may either supply the dollars yourself (explaining that you will collect them back after the exercise is completed) or ask that participants use their own money for the exercise. Be sure to have some extra dollar bills available in case participants do not have cash with them at the session.
2. Explain that the object of this activity is for each participant to negotiate with a partner with the goal of getting the partner's dollar and thereby increasing their own wealth.
3. Tell the participants they will have 10 minutes to negotiate using whatever strategies they decide on. The goal is to win. For example, one person might offer to sell his or her homemade lunch to the partner for the dollar, or a person might offer to type a report or offer some other service for which the partner is willing to pay.
4. Reconvene the group after 10 minutes. If the participants worked with real dollar bills, give the participants a moment to return any bills that changed hands during the exercise to their original owners.

Debriefing Questions:

1. What is your reaction to the activity?
2. Who doubled their money? How did you get it? What strategy did you use?
3. What did you have to give in order to get the wealth you wanted? How did you make your decisions about what to give and what to get?
4. Who defined wealth as something other than money? What other wealth did you acquire?
5. How did your personal values influence your decisions?
6. What does this exercise have to do with diversity?
7. What can you take away from this activity?
e 8. How did you learn about winning and losing as you were growing up? What messages did you receive then?
e 9. Reveal the following questions on the prepared flipchart labeled "Winning, Losing, and Negotiation." Ask the participants to discuss the following questions in small groups at their tables and to designate a reporter who will summarize the themes of their discussion:

   ■ In the workplace, what are some things you have to negotiate and be willing to compromise about?

   ■ What are your "non-negotiable" topics or issues? What are you unwilling to give up or compromise?

   ■ Is it important for the people you work with to know what you will and will not negotiate? Why?

   ■ How can sharing this information about yourself and knowing this information about others help you at work?

Double or Nothing **Continued**

e   10. What does this have to do with diversity?

e   11. What can you take away from this activity?

Key Points:

■   Our negotiating strategies and drives are rooted in various factors that include personality and culture.

■   The importance of winning—or obtaining wealth—is seen differently by both individuals and cultures. The definitions of these words may even vary from culture to culture.

Double or Nothing **Prepared Flipchart**

Winning, Losing, and Negotiating
1. In the workplace, what are some things you have to negotiate and be willing to compromise about?
2. What are your "non-negotiable" topics or issues? What are you unwilling to give up or compromise?
3. Is it important for the people you work with to know what you will and will not negotiate? Why?
4. How can sharing this information about yourself and knowing this information about others help you at work?

Doves or Hawks—Individual Conflict Styles

Time: Basic Activity: 15–20 minutes

Expanded Activity **e** : 30–40 minutes

Equipment: Prepared flipchart

Materials: Prepared (pre-written) posters

Handouts: None

Objective:

- To help participants recognize that people have distinct conflict styles and that being flexible and respecting others can help to resolve conflict

Procedure:

1. Place the prepared posters in various areas of the room.
2. Ask the participants to walk around the room and stand beside the poster that most represents the way they deal with conflict. The participants will gather in groups by the posters.
3. Give each group a marker and ask them to select a group reporter. Direct their attention to the prepared flipchart labeled "Four Questions." Ask them to answer each of the questions as a team and write their answers on the poster. Allow 10 minutes.
4. Do not reconvene. Ask for reports from each group on the themes from their discussion while the groups remain standing in front of their posters.

Debriefing Questions:

1. What did you learn about yourself? About others?
2. How can this information help you work with others in a diverse workplace?
e 3. Ask each group to sit together and select a new reporter. Ask the reporter to be prepared to summarize the themes generated by their group in response to the following two questions:
   - What do you value and respect about each of the other conflict styles?
   - When you work with each of the other styles, how might they influence you to leverage your strengths and avoid potential pitfalls?

   After 10 minutes, reconvene the large group.
e 4. How does this exercise relate to diversity?
e 5. What can you take away from this activity?

Key Points:

- We all have personal styles for dealing with conflict, and each style offers strengths and potential pitfalls.
- By learning behaviors of other styles and incorporating them into interactions with other people, we can more easily and more successfully resolve conflicts.

Doves or Hawks—Individual Conflict Styles **Continued**

Trainer's Notes:

■ When you prepare the four posters that will be displayed around the room, you may wish to add pictures of the animals used to represent the conflict styles. Be sure to leave space on the posters so that the groups will be able to write in the strengths and pitfalls they identify for that style of conflict.

Doves or Hawks—Individual Conflict Styles **Prepared Posters**

Rabbit

Team Name: _____

Animal: Bunny Rabbit

Focus/Motivation: Avoidance

Motto #1: "I'll escape when I have the chance."

Motto #2: _____

_____

Pit Bull

Team Name _____

Animal: Pit Bull

Focus/Motivation: Competition

Motto #1: "Winning is the only thing!"

Motto #2: _____

_____

Worker Bee

Team Name _____

Animal: Worker Bee

Focus/Motivation: Cooperation

Motto # 1: "I'll act for the good of the group."

Motto #2: _____

_____

Chameleon

Team Name _____

Animal: Chameleon

Focus/Motivation: Adaptation

Motto #1: "I'm willing to change to blend in."

Motto #2: _____

_____

Doves or Hawks—Individual Conflict Styles **Prepared Flipchart**

Four Questions

(Following discussion, write your group's responses to these four questions on your poster.)

1. What are the strengths of this conflict style?

2. What are the potential pitfalls of this conflict style?

3. What name will you give your group?

4. What should be this group's second motto?

Kindergarten Incident

Time: Basic Activity: 15–20 minutes   **Expanded Activity** 🄴**:** 30–40 minutes

Equipment: None

Materials: None

Handout: Kindergarten Incident Scenario

Objectives:

- To discuss how to deal with a diversity issue in a community setting
- To acknowledge that personal experiences can affect our behavior at work and that experiences at work can affect our behavior in our personal lives

Procedure:

1. Divide the participants into small discussion groups with four or five people to a group. Ask the groups to appoint a reporter who will lead the discussion and later report to the larger group.
2. Give each participant a copy of the handout.
3. Ask each person to read the scenario, think for a few minutes about the questions listed on the handout, then discuss. Allow 10 minutes for the group to complete the task.
4. Reconvene and ask the groups to report.

Debriefing Questions:

1. If the engineer were your co-worker and shared this story with you, what would you do? How would you demonstrate the Consideration, Appreciation, Respect, and Empathy (C.A.R.E.) Model provided in Chapter 4 in your conversation(s) with your co-worker?
2. In this scenario, what is the best possible outcome for your interaction with your co-worker? How can it be achieved?
3. What can you take away from this activity? (Note: If you are using the Expanded Activity, this question should only be used to close the activity.)
🄴 4. How might your response to your co-worker affect your working relationship?
🄴 5. What challenges are presented by having this discussion in the workplace?

Key Points:

- We do not have the power to control the lives and situations of others, and our power to influence others often is limited.
- Demonstrating consideration, appreciation, respect, and empathy builds connection, cooperation, and trust.

Trainer's Note:

- You may want to use this activity in conjunction with the C.A.R.E. Model provided in Chapter 4. The kindergarten scenario actually occurred as described. In the end, the parents of the children involved had a meeting and explored ways to help their children understand their differences.

Kindergarten Incident **Handout**

Kindergarten Incident Story

You work with an Asian engineer who comes to work upset about a situation that has just occurred with his preschool-age son. Your child attends the same school. It seems that the child came home crying because some kids beat him up and shouted that they didn't like Japanese kids. When the child asked what a "Japanese kid" was, his father explained that their family was not Japanese, but rather Chinese, and told his son to go back to school the next day and tell that to the other children.

The next day, the boy came home, having been beaten up again. The other children had taunted him with a sentence to the effect that, "Chinese or Japanese, you don't belong here."

Consider these events in relation to the following questions:

- What's happening here?
- What might you say to the Chinese engineer?
- What do you think the Chinese engineer should do?
- Because your child goes to the same school, should you do anything? If so, what?
- What about the child's teacher?

Chapter 11
Team Building

Diversity: the art of thinking independently together.
MALCOLM S. FORBES

Building a high-functioning team involves processes for setting and defining goals, establishing roles, making decisions, developing a plan, and carrying it out. These teams can take various forms, such as traditional workgroups, impromptu short-term teams, special-purpose teams, cross-functional teams, self-managed teams, and virtual teams.

While ensuring diversity among team members is generally recognized as an important way of ensuring creative and effective outcomes, it also is important to know how to leverage that diversity to achieve the desired goals.

This section presents activities you can use to explore ways of building teams that optimize their diversity and enhance inclusiveness.

Understanding Commitment

Time: Basic Activity: 15–20 minutes   **Expanded Exercise** [e]: 30–40 minutes

Equipment: None

Materials: Prepared flipchart

Handouts: None

Objectives:

- To define commitment
- To explore behaviors associated with commitment
- To increase participants' awareness of how they react to people who express commitment in ways different from their own

Procedure:

1. Let participants know that commitment is the focus of this activity. Direct them to form groups of four people.
2. Let the participants know that the activity will use the institution of marriage as the object of inquiry about commitment and how it shapes behavior.
3. Ask them to consider the situation of a person who has been married and divorced six or seven times. (While there are some celebrities who have that sort of marital history, there are also non-famous people with that sort of history.) Ask them to silently notice their internal response to the question "How would you describe the level of commitment of such a person to the institution of marriage and why?"
4. Direct participants to take turns answering that question in their small groups. Each person will have exactly 1 minute to answer the question. If a person's answer requires less than 1 minute, direct the participants to remain silent until it is the next person's turn. As facilitator, give the participants a clear signal each time 1 minute is up. During each person's turn to speak, the other three people in the group simply listen. Only one person will talk at a time in the groups for next 4 minutes.
5. After the last 1-minute turn, reconvene the large group.
6. Ask the participants to share what they heard from each other without saying who said what. Encourage the expression of different points of view. There is no right or wrong response. Point out that while opinions differ on this topic, everyone's point of view is shaped by individual beliefs, values, and experiences.
7. Ask the participants to name the behaviors identified as indicating commitment to marriage. If they have trouble coming up with ideas, suggest some behaviors, such as engagement, fidelity, or planning for a future together
8. Record the participants' responses on a flipchart labeled "Marriage: Behaviors that Indicate Commitment."
9. Present the prepared flipchart with the *Webster's Dictionary* definition of commitment. Ask the participants how this definition compares to their discussion and their ideas.
10. Ask the participants to direct their attention from commitment and marriage to commitment and teamwork.
11. Ask each small group to select a recorder and reporter and to brainstorm a list of behaviors that indicate commitment to teamwork. Allow 5 minutes.
12. Reconvene the group and ask each reporter to share the ideas from their group round-robin style. Get two ideas from one team, then two ideas from the next team, and so on through the last team. Then begin the cycle again. Record each behavior named on a flipchart labeled "Teamwork: Behaviors that Indicate Commitment."
13. Direct participants to repeat the above process to address a different question, "What behaviors indicate commitment to diversity and inclusion?" Allow 5 minutes.

Understanding Commitment Continued

14. Reconvene the group and let participants know that you will ask the teams to share their team's ideas round-robin style, as before. Let the reporters know that they don't need to share duplicate behaviors.
15. Record each named behavior on a flipchart labeled "Teamwork: Behaviors that Indicate Diversity."
16. Wrap up the activity by asking some debriefing questions.

Debriefing Questions:

1. What do you notice when you compare the actions listed on each chart?
2. What are some examples of "walking the talk" with respect to commitment? What is the effect of doing this?
3. What are some examples of people paying lip service to a commitment? What is the effect of doing this?
4. How does this discussion apply to situations at work?
5. What can you take away from this exercise?
6. What must be in place for you to be committed to a person? A project? An organization?
7. When those criteria are present, how do you benefit? What about other team members? The project? The organization?
8. When those criteria are absent, what challenges do you face in contributing 100 percent of your capacity?
9. How do you overcome those challenges?
10. When you do not overcome the challenges, what are some of the consequences for you, for others, for projects, or for the organization?
11. How might this exercise affect you when you return to your work?

Key Points:

- Our definitions and levels of commitment are influenced by our values, beliefs, and experiences.
- Our values, beliefs, and experiences shape the lens through which we see and judge the behavior of others.
- Individual and cultural differences may influence what people are willing to commit to and the degree of that commitment. For example, for some people family obligations, religious practices, loyalty, and individual priorities may take precedence over a work commitment. For other people, work always comes first.
- People have different ways of demonstrating commitment. It may be important to discuss expectations with respect to behaviors that indicate commitment.

Trainer's Notes:

- Participants may bring up the question of whether marriage is the only way to convey and express commitment to a relationship. That may be an interesting discussion but it is not the focus of this exercise.

Understanding Commitment **Prepared Flipchart**

Commitment Is
Webster's Third New International Dictionary (Merriam-Webster Inc., 2000) defines commitment as "a decisive moral choice that involves a person in a definite course of action."

Optimizing Team Diversity

Time: Basic Activity: 15 minutes   **Expanded Exercise** e: 30 minutes

Equipment: Prepared flipcharts

Materials: Pens or Pencils and Paper for Participants

Handout: Team Diversity Assessment

Objectives:

- To examine behaviors that optimize the diversity of team members
- To identify behaviors that help to identify biases and assumptions that limit team performance
- e To provide a team diversity assessment that can be used in the workplace to assess team effectiveness

Procedure:

1. Explain that this activity offers team members the opportunity to examine their own perspectives in relation to diversity issues.
2. Pair up the participants and show Prepared Flipchart #1.
3. Tell the participants to consider the diverse team actions listed on the flipchart. Ask the pairs to discuss how the actions listed can make a difference in team performance.
4. Instruct the pairs to come up with additional helpful actions and write them down. Allow 5 to 10 minutes.
5. Ask the pairs to call out their additions to the list. Add them to the flipchart.
6. e Divide the group into small groups of four to six people. Assign a reporter to each group.
7. e Divide the expanded list of actions listed on the flipchart equally among the groups.
8. e Tell groups to brainstorm situations in which they could practice the behaviors assigned to their group. Allow 7 minutes.
9. e Distribute the Team Diversity Assessment handout and ask the participants to complete the form individually with respect to a team they are a member of. Tell the participants their responses will be kept confidential.
10. e Reconvene the large group and ask the groups to report out their discussion.

Debriefing Questions:

1. What thoughts or feelings do you have about this exercise?
2. What can you take away from this exercise that will help you be more successful working on your team(s)?
3. e What did you learn or confirm about yourself? About diversity? About being an effective team member?
4. e What did you learn from the team diversity assessment?
5. e How might you apply your insights from this activity to your day-to-day life with teams at work?

Key Points:

- Specific behaviors promote and erode team effectiveness. This exercise looked at positive behaviors. Some examples of behaviors that erode team effectiveness in terms of diversity include telling jokes that get a laugh at the expense of an identified group, mocking accents, ignoring younger or older team members, and so forth.
- Effective communication, clear goals, and clear lines of accountability are essential to effective teamwork in any situation.

Optimizing Team Diversity Continued

Trainer's Notes:

- Here are some optional additional steps in conducting the expanded version of this activity.

1. Tell participants that now that they have applied the Team Diversity Assessment to a team they belong to, they will have an opportunity to assess their individual contributions to each item on the assessment. The purpose of this step is to increase awareness of their strengths and identify development areas so the participants can improve their ability to contribute in ways that optimize team diversity.

2. Tell the participants you won't ask them to share their self-assessment with anyone. Show Prepared Flipchart #2. Review the self-evaluation rating system, making the following statements:

   - "Review your list. Put a double plus beside the actions that people have told you that you do and that they value."

   - "Put a single plus beside actions that you think you do but that have not been acknowledged for. This may reflect four things: (1) others don't think it is a strength; (2) you haven't used it recently; (3) the way you've used it hasn't had a positive effect; or (4) you have the strength and it has been noticed but not acknowledged."

   - "Put a star beside the actions that you know you can improve."

   Allow the participants 2 to 3 minutes to complete the self-assessment.

3. Close the extended activity by asking each participant to share one action they will take.

Optimizing Team Diversity Prepared Flipchart #1

Optimizing Team Diversity

- Create a safe environment.
- Look beyond first impressions.
- Pronounce names correctly.
- Seek different perspectives.
- Discuss diversity issues openly.

Optimizing Team Diversity **Prepared Flipchart #2**

Optimizing Team Diversity
++ = Acknowledged Strength
+   = Unacknowledged Strength
*   = Development Opportunity

Optimizing Team Diversity Handout

Team Diversity Assessment

Check the appropriate box where

(1) = Strongly disagree, (2) = Disagree, (3) = Neither agree nor disagree, (4) = Agree, and (5) = Strongly agree.

	1	2	3	4	5
1. Our team has a stated vision.					
2. The vision is accepted by all.					
3. The vision is understood by all.					
4. Our team includes reference to diversity.					
5. Our team considers the values and needs of each of its members.					
6. Our team environment supports diversity.					
7. Our team encourages members to be open with one another.					
8. Team members help one another.					
9. Our team promotes the sharing of success.					
10. Our team encourages individual interaction across diversity lines.					
11. The team members are open to differences of opinion.					
12. There is appreciation of the talents and skills of each individual.					
13. Members can count on one another, irrespective of their diverse background.					
14. The team is able to deal with interpersonal problems and conflicts.					
15. Team members feel secure in bringing up problems and conflicts.					
16. Team members can determine whether their problems are diversity-related.					
17. There is a system in place for addressing problems and conflicts.					

From *Team Building for Diverse Work Groups* by Selma Myers. Copyright 1996 by Richard Chang Associates, Inc. Reprinted by permission of the publisher.

Chapter 12
Energizers

Become a fixer, not just a fixture.
ANTHONY J. D'ANGELO

Whether designing a series of activities for a workshop or conducting a lengthy meeting, it is valuable to use a variety of activities to quickly energize the group.

Energizers can be useful in various situations: when the group is unresponsive; when people need an opportunity to lighten up after a difficult or tense discussion; or when it would be helpful to reinvigorate creativity and discussion

It is natural for participants to get tired as a result of being in workshop or a meeting, whether it lasts a half day or a full day. The overall pacing of a session is one aspect to take into consideration when developing the agenda.

Including a combination of regular breaks (some facilitators offer participants in full-day workshops a 10-minute break after every hour of meeting time) and energizers along with a variety of activities that involve lots of participation will help people maintain their energy and be more receptive to new information, discussion, and skill development.

This section presents activities you can use to quickly energize a group.

And the Winner Is …!

Time: Basic Activity: 5–10 minutes

Equipment: None

Materials: Pen or pencil and one index card for each participant

Handouts: None

Objectives:

- To quickly identify commonalities and differences among participants
- To create ongoing energy, excitement and fun

Procedure:

1. Distribute a writing instrument and one index card to each participant.
2. Tell the participants to take 5 minutes to write three things about themselves that most others in the room don't know. For example: you might write down the city, state, or country you were born in; how many working television sets you have in any property you have—your home, recreational vehicle, and so forth; if you are a twin; if you ride horses; if you have taught a sport, or other personal information.
3. Collect the completed index cards.
4. When you have collected all the index cards, choose two or three from the entire stack. Read one item from each card. Note: If you have a small group, read only two items in this first round. If you have a larger group, you may elect to read three or even four items in the first round.
5. Tell the participants to stand up if what you read applies to them, even if they didn't write it on their index cards. Applaud for the people standing. Allow everyone to notice how many people stand for each item. Invite the participants to make brief comments if they choose to. Continue until all the items identified in this first round have been read and people have stood and been acknowledged. Check the items off as you go and be careful not to repeat categories.
6. Tell the participants that throughout the day from time-to-time, you'll read two or three more items so they can continue learning what they have in common with each other.
7. Repeat rounds just before or after breaks or any time you need to energize the room.
8. Be sure to conduct enough rounds so that you acknowledge every category written on the index cards. After the first round, during the first exercise in which participants are working on their own, go through the entire stack of index cards to eliminate duplications, tweak words, count the categories, and determine how many rounds you'll need and how many categories you'll address during each round.

Debriefing Questions:

1. After items from all the categories have been acknowledged, ask participants what they learned from the ongoing exercise. Ask what surprised them.
2. How might the participants use what they learned or even use this exercise in their organization?

Key Points:

- We can learn some important things about each other quickly, and we can have fun while doing it.
- Both commonalities and differences can be interesting.

Pulse Check

Time: Basic Activity: 10–15 minutes   **Expanded Exercise e:** 20–25 minutes

Equipment: Prepared flipchart

Materials: 3" x 5" Index Cards

Handouts: None

Objectives:

- To assess the comfort level of workshop participants and give them a way of expressing that comfort level
- To increase participants' comfort in talking about challenging material
- To raise the energy of the group

Procedure:

1. Explain that this exercise is a way to determine how participants feel about dealing with the topic of diversity in today's work-place.
2. Divide the participants into small groups and give each person a blank 3" x 5" index card. Ask each group to appoint a reporter.
3. Tell the participants their task is to note on the cards their feelings, concerns, and thoughts regarding the workshop they are about to begin or one that they have been participating in. Also ask them to write down one or two specific diversity topics that they find challenging.
4. Ask each reporter to gather the cards, shuffle them, and read them aloud to the small group. Direct each small group to discuss the similarities and differences they heard as their cards were read out loud.
5. After 5 to 10 minutes, ask each group's reporter to summarize the general results of their discussion. Record the themes from the report-outs on the flipchart. Say that this is a snapshot of feelings and thoughts in the room right now; it may or may not be the same in a couple hours if we take another snapshot. As with any other subject, people's perspectives and feelings about diversity topics often change in the course of discussion and with reflection.
6. Thank the participants for sharing their concerns and feelings and for listening respectfully to those of others.
e 7. Tell the participants that you want to continue to build on their discussion to identify and agree on some learning guidelines for the session. Tell them these guidelines will help create a relatively safe environment for honest discussion and sharing in order to deepen the group's learning about diversity and inclusion.
e 8. Reveal the Learning Behavioral Guidelines flipchart.
e 9. Ask what other behaviors must be demonstrated to encourage learning and honest discussion. Write their suggestions (using active and positive language) on the flipchart.
e 10. After behaviors have been identified and explained, ask participants for their commitment to demonstrating the behaviors. If yes, continue. If no, address the concern and make whatever adjustments are necessary to the list.

Debriefing Questions:

1. What makes our feelings and concerns change?
2. How do feelings affect participation, learning, and people in the workshop?
3. How do feelings affect staff meetings, team meetings, or departmental meetings?
4. What makes you comfortable or uncomfortable sharing feelings?

Pulse Check **Continued**

5. What can you take away from the exercise?

[e] 6. What have you learned so far that will help you create and sustain an environment in which everyone is valued, respected, and heard?

Key Points:

■ For everyone to be able to participate freely and contribute their best, they must feel valued, respected, and heard.

■ Communication can identify what promotes and erodes those feelings.

■ Today we are talking about topics that are not usually addressed in many contexts. Doing this may create some discomfort but it also makes it possible to gain more awareness and understanding of differences that are in the workplace today.

Pulse Check **Prepared Flipchart**

Learning Behavioral Guidelines

- ■ Demonstrate respect
- ■ Participant actively
- ■ Keep confidences
- ■ Honor the speaker—no side conversations
- ■ Agree or disagree respectfully
- ■ Have fun

How Do You Say "Hello"?

Time: Basic Activity: 15–20 minutes   **Expanded Activity** ⓔ: 45–60 minutes

Equipment: None

Materials: Prepared paper slips with greetings from the handout and a basket or other container

Handout: How Do You Say "Hello"?

Objective:

■ To raise awareness of greeting patterns and key phrases in different languages

Procedure:

1. Begin the session by saying "Hello" using any one of the greetings listed on the attached handout. If you receive no response, repeat the greeting or try a more familiar one. (Responses may be different depending on whether the group is familiar with the particular greeting. More obscure languages may bring out different responses.)

2. Comment on any responses. Discuss how people felt when a greeting was familiar or perhaps totally foreign to them.

3. Point out that there are also nonverbal greetings. Ask participants to think about nonverbal greetings in which body language is the most significant element. Ask them to describe familiar nonverbal greetings or any experiences they have had with nonverbal greetings. (If necessary, make some suggestions, such as bowing, shaking hands, hugging, kissing, and so forth.)

4. Ask the participants to add any other international greetings they are familiar with or any experiences they have had with them. Explain that later they will be given a list of verbal and nonverbal greetings in other languages.

5. Put slips of paper with greeting words from the handout in a container, such as a hat or basket, and ask each participant to draw one. Tell the participants to silently read the phrases on the slips of paper and then use the phrases to greet four or five of the other participants.

Debriefing Questions:

1. What is your reaction to this activity?

2. What did you learn?

3. What are the benefits of knowing basic words and phrases of other countries or cultures, or even of American cultures different from our own? How might knowing such words or phrases benefit your professional life? Your personal life?

4. What are some benefits to your organization of being multilingual?

ⓔ 5. Pass out the handout and suggest that participants learn a few unfamiliar greetings. Also suggest that they expand the list by talking with people from different countries and cultures.

ⓔ 6. Tell participants to write other key words and phrases they need to know how to say in different languages so they can be more successful in their interactions with people of different cultures. Next, tell them to identify a person or people with whom they can consult to learn how to say each word or phrase properly.

ⓔ 7. Tell participants to write key words and phrases from their own culture that they would like to share with others to help them be more successful in their interactions.

ⓔ 8. Tell participants to prioritize both lists and create timelines for the action plans they developed in steps 1 and 2.

How Do You Say "Hello"? **Continued**

Key Points:

- People whose primary language is different from ours usually appreciate it when we exert the interest, time, and energy to learn a few basic words and phrases in their primary language.
- In the global market, organizations and teams are increasingly multilingual. As individuals, teams, and organizations, we benefit most by leveraging this skill and learning about different cultures.

How Do You Say "Hello"?

Portuguese—Good day	Bom die (bowng JEE-a)
Bulgarian—Good day	Dobar den
Danish—Good morning	God morgen (go MOHRN)
Tagalog—Good morning	Magandang umaga po (a-gahn-DAHNG oo-MA-ga-PO)
Arabic—Peace upon you (traditional Arab greeting)	Salaam alaykum
Italian—Good day	Buon giorno (bwohn JOR-no)
German—Good day	Guten Tag (GOO-tun TAHK)
Japanese—Good morning	Ohayoo gozaimasu (ohio go-zai-mahss)
Mandarin—How do you do?	Ni hau ma? (NEE how mah?)
Spanish—Good day	Buenos días (Boy nus dee us)
French—Hello	Bonjour (bohn-zhoor)
Dutch—Good morning	Goedemorgen (gue-duh-mor-ghen)
Shona (Zimbabwe)—Good morning	Mangwanani
Thai—Hello (said by women)	Sawadi kha
Thai—Hello (said by men)	Sawadi khrap

How Do You Say "Hello" Handout **Continued**

Nonverbal Greetings

In many countries, a handshake is commonly used in greeting. However, you should be aware that there are many other nonverbal greetings. A few examples are listed below. Add any additional ones that you know of.

- In Malaysia, when greeting close friends, a man uses both hands to grasp the hand of the other.
- People from India, Sri Lanka, and Bangladesh greet each other by placing their own palms together under the chin and bowing slightly.
- Kissing practices vary and include men kissing each other in greeting, sometimes two or three times and on different cheeks. In some Asian countries, if a boy hugs and kisses a girl in public, he insults her.
- In Taiwan, a nod of one's head is considered appropriate when meeting someone for the first time. For acquaintances and close friends, a handshake is most common.

Chapter 13
Closing Up

Always do right. This will gratify some people and astonish the rest.
MARK TWAIN

At the end of a workshop, participants benefit by following a process that helps them begin digesting and integrating what they learned during the session. This process has two main components.

The first component is an opportunity for the participants to reflect privately and map out a personal action plan. Creating the action plan will help them identify ways to apply new insights, skills, and knowledge to their daily lives.

These actions don't have to be major—though they can be. They must, however, be achievable, with just a little stretch, in view of the participant's current reality and competing priorities. The participants also must see some benefit to themselves in taking these actions.

The second component is an opportunity for the participants to talk among themselves about what they learned and what they will do. These conversations create another learning opportunity that focuses on how colleagues integrate and apply new learning. It also strengthens the participants' sense of accountability and determination to follow up on the actions they talk about. Some facilitators like to end their workshops by creating a buddy system, having participants exchange contact information and schedule follow-up meetings.

This section presents activities you can use to help participants integrate learning, create action plans, and end the session in a positive, reinforcing way.

Setting New Directions

Time: Basic Activity: 10–15 minutes   **Expanded Activity e:** 20–30 minutes

Equipment: Prepared flipchart

Materials: None

Handout: e Setting New Directions: Challenges and Solutions

Objectives:

■ To establish some general guidelines for the future in relation to diversity at work
■ To explore some of the concerns participants might have in reaching those goals

Procedure:

1. Divide the participants into small groups and ask them to appoint a reporter. Explain that to fully leverage diversity and strengthen inclusion, it is helpful to take some time to identify changes that would support those goals in their organization.

2. Ask the participants to take 5 minutes to brainstorm and discuss answers to the question on the prepared flipchart:
   ■ What changes in your organization would you like to see in the next 90 days? (Give specific examples.)

3. After 5 minutes, ask the reporter for each group to report two suggestions. As you proceed, ask the groups not to repeat anything that's already been said. Record each group's suggestions on a flipchart. Continue this process until all the groups' suggestions have been identified and recorded.

e   4. Divide the participants into small groups. Ask them to look at the list of changes they have identified, thinking of them as challenges and assessing whether any of the challenges are interconnected.

5. Evenly assign the listed challenges to the groups, making sure that the groups address different challenges from each other. Usually each group will have up to three challenges. If challenges are related, try to assign the related challenges to the same group.

e   6. Tell the groups to use the Setting New Directions: Challenges and Solutions handout for the next phase of the activity. Ask them to write their assigned challenges in the boxes on the left-hand side of the page.

e   7. Ask each group to discuss and come to agreement on whether or not they have control over the challenges assigned to their group. If the group's answer is "yes," they should check the appropriate box in the "controllable" column and to brainstorm solutions. Ask them to write their ideas in the boxes in the right-hand column. If the group's answer is "no," they should consider what aspects of that challenge they can influence. Direct the groups to brainstorm those solutions and write them in the boxes in the right-hand column.

e   8. Tell the participants they have 5 to 10 minutes to address their assigned challenges using the handout. Note: If groups have one challenge, give them 5 minutes; if they have two challenges, give them 7 minutes; if they have three challenges, give them 10 minutes.

e   9. After 5 to 10 minutes, have each group report.

e   10. Encourage participants to record each challenge and its suggested solutions on their copies of the handout so they will have a record of the ideas generated by the group.

Setting New Directions **Continued**

Debriefing Questions:

1. What feelings or thoughts do you have about this activity?
2. Why is it important to establish goals and direction with respect to valuing diversity and increasing inclusion?
3. What can you do to positively affect your organization? Consider what you can influence as well as what you can control.
4. What do you take away from this activity?
5. Please share one way you will contribute to efforts to leverage diversity and increase inclusion in their organization.

Key Points:

■ Achieving any goal requires clear objectives and action plans. Goals associated with diversity initiatives and strategies are no different.

■ Each individual has a role to play in creating and sustaining environments in which everyone values diversity and inclusion.

Trainer's Notes:

■ An optional way to conduct this activity is to divide the participants into small groups, give each group flipchart paper and markers, and have them record their suggestions on the flipchart paper. Tell the groups they will need to select both a scribe and a reporter, and allow them 5 minutes to brainstorm and record their suggestions. After 5 minutes, ask the groups to post their lists. Ask each reporter to present his or her group's list. Tell the participants to identify one or two solutions they will use to demonstrate that they value diversity and inclusion.

Setting New Directions Handout

Challenges and Solutions

Challenges	Controllable		Solutions
	Yes	No	

Time Waits for No One

Time: Basic Activity: 15–20 minutes   **Expanded Activity** 🄴**:** 25–30 minutes

Equipment: Prepared Flipchart

Materials: None

Handouts: None

Objective:

- ■ To have participants plan a timeline for addressing diversity issues and give them a chance to think about what can be done in any given period of time

Procedure:

1. Set up small discussion groups and appoint a leader or reporter (same person) for each group. Ask the participants to discuss what they can do to help their organization's diversity efforts succeed. Ask the groups to think about different approaches based on different time segments as shown on the flipchart. For example, they might suggest creating a diversity newsletter as a long-term project, or taking a few minutes simply to talk to new employees and make them feel welcome as a short-term project. Allow 10 to 15 minutes for the discussion.
2. Reconvene and take about 5 minutes to have each group report. Record the various suggestions on the appropriate time segments on the flipchart.
🄴 3. Tell the small groups to spend the next 10 minutes continuing to work with the lists they have developed. This time, they will identify actions they can take as individuals to demonstrate support for each of the ideas from the first part of the activity. Tell them to select a different reporter.
🄴 4. After 10 minutes, ask the groups to report. Tell the participants to listen for actions they can take and that they will be asked to identify one thing that they will commit to do to demonstrate they value diversity and inclusion.

Debriefing Questions:

1. What are your reactions to this activity?
2. Given what you've learned here today, what will you do to demonstrate valuing diversity and inclusion?
🄴 3. What did you learn or confirm about yourself? About diversity and diversity initiatives or strategies?

Key Points:

- ■ Accomplishing any goal requires development of an action plan. Goals associated with diversity initiatives and strategies are no different.
- ■ Each individual has a role to play in creating and sustaining environments where everyone values diversity and inclusion.

Trainer's Notes:

- ■ An optional way of conducting this activity is to first ask the large group to identify current organizational departments, processes, and activities that can be leveraged to positively affect valuing diversity and increasing inclusion. (Examples might include Human Resources, marketing, or a bi-weekly newsletter.) Then divide the participants into small groups, assign items from the list to each group, give each group flipchart paper, and allow them to scribe their own suggestions.

Time Waits for No One **Prepared Flipchart**

Here is a sample of the timelines that can be put on the prepared flipchart. Adjust them as appropriate for the group and the organization.

Timelines
■ 60 seconds to 60 minutes
■ 1 hour to 24 hours
■ 1 week to 1 month
■ 3 months to 6 months
■ 1 year or more

Words of Wisdom

Time: Basic Activity: 10–15 minutes   **Expanded Activity** **e**: 20–25 minutes

Equipment: Flipchart

Materials:

- Enough Chinese fortune cookies for each participant
- Three slips of paper for each participant
- **e** ■ An additional two slips of paper for each participant

Handouts: None

Objective:

- To explore the qualities a person needs to be successful in working with diversity

Procedure:

1. Pass out a fortune cookie and a small strip of paper to each participant and explain that this activity is about creating "Words of Wisdom" in dealing with diversity.
2. Direct the participants to think of a phrase or sentence in fortune-cookie style and write it on one of the slips of paper. Fortune-cookie style usually has a structure like "She who (some positive action or quality) is (some positive action or quality)." For example:
   - He who is a *good listener* has a genuine *advantage* in *building relations* across cultures.
   - She who shows *patience* with people who may have different views *succeeds* in building rapport.
   - He who is *open-minded has great success* in working with people who bring different values to work.
3. Allow participants 5 minutes to come up with their fortune-cookie statements.
4. Ask for volunteers to read their statements. As they do, record the qualities named in each statement on the flipchart. Lead a discussion regarding these qualities and how important they are in dealing with diversity. As for the cookies, enjoy them!
5. **e** Pass out a second strip of paper to each participant.
6. **e** Tell the participants they'll repeat the activity, but this time they should write one thing they will find ways of sharing with others about the benefit of valuing diversity and inclusion. Give the participants 3 minutes to think of and write their statements.
7. **e** After 3 minutes, ask for volunteers to read their statements. As they do, record them on a second flipchart page labeled "Benefits."

Debriefing Questions:

1. What are your reactions to this activity?
2. What did you learn or confirm about diversity and how each of us contributes and is affected by it?
3. Ask the participants what they can take away from this activity and how they will apply it in the workplace.

Key Points:

- To create and sustain an environment in which all people are respected, valued, and heard, everyone will have to be actively involved and supportive.
- We can all quickly think of at least one action we can take to demonstrate our support for diversity.

Chapter 14
Resources

A journey of a thousand miles must begin with a single step.
LAO TZU

This section presents information about five types of resources, as follows:

- A list of diversity quotations and suggestions for how to use them.

- A list of Web sites to help you stay current with research, new books, and other products related to diversity.

- A set of templates for written communications that you can use to customize announcements for workshops, brown-bag lunches, or meetings, and templates for other diversity-related tasks such as identifying people to help facilitate a workshop and assessing facilitation competencies.

- Suggestions for how to creatively select "volunteers".

- A list of the materials included on the CD-ROM.

Quotable Quotes and How to Use Them

The beauty of including quotations is the wisdom and wit they offer. Traditionally, quotations have been used as a quick way to bring insight and new understanding to any number of different topics. Thought-provoking quotations can provide a unique approach to a complex topic such as diversity.

Quotations are ideal for activities because of their brevity. Using a short quotation is an excellent way to emphasize a point while avoiding a long lecture. Coping with group dynamics and the need to hold participants' interest calls for constantly evaluating material, and quotations offer an interesting way to approach or review some general aspects of diversity.

Many of the quotations we have selected also may offer participants short-cuts to understanding. We hope that the concept of using quotations will help you reach the essence of your message in a brief and interesting way and also explore some of the depth of diversity training.

Using quotations allows participants to learn about and experience dealing with diversity in a variety of ways, promoting a healthy discussion and exchange of ideas about specific diversity issues.

Useful quotations come from politicians, theorists, the theater, novels, speeches, songs, advertisements, and many other sources. They often come from people who are well known, are rarely time-sensitive, and may provide just the right word or phrase to encapsulate the ideas or points you are trying to make in your training sessions.

The quotations presented in this section are easy to use. They have been selected to cover a broad range of subjects, offer universal meaning, and appeal to participants spanning several generations.

Here are some suggestions for using quotations effectively in activities.

- Post some quotations around the room. Ask participants to go around the room and read them and then to stand by the quotation they think would be most interesting to discuss. As the participants gather in groups by the posted quotations, ask that they talk about how they can relate the quotation they selected to some work they are doing or to some diversity issue they encounter in everyday life. Allow the participants a few minutes to talk and then ask each group to report out.

- Distribute a fortune cookie to each participant. Ask the participants to read their fortunes and then to select from a list of quotations (either posted on a flip chart or provided on a handout) the one they think is worth remembering in terms of diversity. Suggest that the participants write their chosen quotations on the back of their fortune-cookie slip, and then ask each participant to read aloud the one they selected. A more detailed version of this activity is described in the Fortune Cookie Exercise.

■ Select as many quotations as there are participants in the group. Put the quotations on slips of paper in a basket or hat and pass them around. Ask each participant to take one, study it, and report out how the concept can be put to work at his or her job or in his or her everyday life.

■ Give each participant a list of quotations along with some paper and crayons. Ask the participants to pick out one quotation and draw a picture of how it might relate to their lives or their work in dealing with diversity.

■ Pair up participants and ask them to look over their list of quotations. Have each participant pick out a quotation from someone with whom he or she might be familiar. Ask the participant to discuss what is known about the life of the person who said or wrote the selected quotation and why that particular quotation is important.

■ Bring newspaper pages (of any date) to distribute to the participants. Ask the group to peruse the various articles to see how many quotable sentences they find. Have the participants determine the people responsible for the quotations they select and discuss with a partner how the quotes might affect their work or relationship to diversity.

■ On the cover sheet of a handout packet, choose several quotes that most closely address a diversity issue you plan to talk about with the group. Use one or two of the quotations as the opening for your icebreaker.

Quotable Quotes

"Wow" Quotes

It is a great shock at the age of five or six to find that in a world of Gary Coopers you are the Indian.
JAMES BALDWIN

We send missionaries to China so the Chinese can get to heaven, but we won't let them into our country.
PEARL S. BUCK

A fanatic is one who can't change his mind and won't change the subject.
SIR WINSTON CHURCHILL

A great many people think they are thinking when they are merely rearranging their prejudices.
WILLIAM JAMES

Bigotry is the disease of ignorance, of morbid minds; enthusiasm of the free and buoyant. Education and free discussion are the antidotes of both.
THOMAS JEFFERSON

Don't compromise yourself. You are all you've got.
JANIS JOPLIN

We aren't what we ought to be, we aren't what we should be, we aren't even what we could be, but thank God we're not what we were.
MARTIN LUTHER KING

Be sincere; be brief; be seated.
FRANKLIN D. ROOSEVELT

The one absolute certain way to bring this nation to ruin....would be to permit it to become a tangle of squabbling nationalities.
THEODORE ROOSEVELT

One day our descendants will think it incredible that we paid so much attention to things like the amount of melanin in our skin or the shape of our eyes or our gender instead of the unique identities of each of us as complex human beings.
FRANKLIN THOMAS

It were not best that we should all think alike; it is difference of opinion that makes horse races.
MARK TWAIN

The constitution does not provide for first and second class citizens.
WENDELL WILKIE

For those who have seen the Earth from space, and for the hundreds and perhaps thousands more who will, the experience most certainly changes your perspective. The things that we share in our world are far more valuable than those which divide us.
DONALD WILLIAMS

Positives about Culture

Diversity is the one true thing we all have in common. Celebrate it every day.
ANONYMOUS

There can be no assumption that today's majority is "right" and the Amish or others like them are "wrong." A way of life that is odd or even erratic but interferes with no right or interests of others is not to be condemned because it is different.
WARREN E. BURGER

We have become not a melting pot but a beautiful mosaic. Different people, different beliefs, different yearnings, different hopes, different dreams.
JIMMY CARTER

The essential philosophic quest in the world is for integration— which is to say, the need to bring together rational philosophy, spiritual belief, scientific knowledge, personal experience, and direct observation into an organic whole.
NORMAN COUSINS, THE CELEBRATION OF LIFE

Human diversity makes tolerance more than a virtue; it makes it a requirement for survival.
RENE DUBOS, CELEBRATIONS OF LIFE, 1981

In the matter of religion, people eagerly fasten their eyes on the difference between their own creed and yours; whilst the charm of the study is in finding the agreements and identities in all the religions of humanity.
RALPH WALDO EMERSON

Quotable Quotes Continued

Diversity: the art of thinking independently together.

MALCOLM S. FORBES

Religions are many and diverse, but reason and goodness are one.

ELBERT HUBBARD

If we cannot end now our differences, at least we can help make the world safe for diversity.

JOHN F. KENNEDY

As long as the differences and diversities of mankind exist, democracy must allow for compromise, for accommodation, and for the recognition of differences.

EUGENE McCARTHY

If we are to achieve a richer culture, rich in contrasting values, we must recognize the whole gamut of human potentialities, and so weave a less arbitrary social fabric, one in which each diverse human gift will find a fitting place.

MARGARET MEAD

It is the duty of every cultured man or woman to read sympathetically the scriptures of the world. If we are to respect others' religions as we would have them respect our own, a friendly study of the world's religions is a sacred duty.

MOHANDAS K. GANDHI

There never was in the world two opinions alike, no more than two hairs or two grains; the most universal quality is diversity.

MONTAIGNE, OF THE RESEMBLANCE OF
CHILDREN TO THEIR FATHERS

The price of the democratic way of life is a growing appreciation of people's differences, not merely as tolerable, but as the essence of a rich and rewarding human experience.

JEROME NATHANSON

There are many paths to enlightenment. Be sure to take one with a heart.

LAO TZU, ENLIGHTENMENT (30)

Perseverance

If you believe you're right...stand up and fight for your place in the sun. If you believe you can do it, hang in for the whole 15 rounds because even if you don't win, you will have earned the respect of everyone in the fight, including yourself, and in that sense you will have prevailed.

ERIN BROCKOVICH

Never, never, never quit.

SIR WINSTON CHURCHILL

Just don't give up trying to do what you really want to do. Where there is love and inspiration, I don't think you can go wrong.

ELLA FITZGERALD

To accomplish great things, we must not only act but also dream, not only plan but also believe.

ANATOLE FRANCE

Don't give up.

ANNE FRANK

I will persist until I succeed. Always will I take another step. If that is of no avail I will take another, and yet another. In truth, one step at a time is not too difficult...I know that small attempts, repeated, will complete any undertaking.

OG MANDINO

Potential or Possibilities

What's possible exceeds what's impossible. Think about it. Do all you can do that is possible today, and in your tomorrow, what was impossible will be possible.

MARK VICTOR HANSEN

Everybody can be great...because anybody can serve. You don't have to have a college degree to serve. You don't have to make your subject and verb agree to serve. You only need a heart full of grace. A soul generated by love.

MARTIN LUTHER KING, JR.

We know what we are, but know not what we may be.

WILLIAM SHAKESPEARE

Quotable Quotes Continued

Taking Action

Be not afraid of going slowly; be only afraid of standing still.
CHINESE PROVERB

What we have to do is to find a way to celebrate our diversity and debate our differences without fracturing our communities.
HILLARY RODHAM CLINTON

To sit back and do nothing is to cooperate with the oppressor.
JANE ELLIOT

You can do anything in life you set your mind to, provided it is powered by your heart.
DOUG FIREBAUGH

Do what's right. Do it right. Do it right now.
BARRY FORBES

Between saying and doing many a pair of shoes is worn out.
ITALIAN PROVERB

Between the great things we cannot do and the small things we will not do, the danger is that we shall do nothing.
ADOLPH MONOD

Nothing is more powerful for your future than being a gatherer of good ideas and information. That's called doing your homework.
JIM ROHN

Learn how to separate the majors and the minors. A lot of people don't do well simply because they major in minor things.
JIM ROHN

To reach a port, we must sail—sail, not tie at anchor—sail, not drift.
FRANKLIN D. ROOSEVELT

Do what you can with what you have where you are.
THEODORE ROOSEVELT

The law of forced efficiency says that there is always enough time to do the most important things.
BRIAN TRACY

A journey of a thousand miles must begin with a single step.
LAO-TSU

Do all the good you can, by all the means you can, in all the ways you can, in all the places you can, at all the times you can, to all the people you can, as long as ever you can.
JOHN WESLEY

Hope

Civilization is a slow process of adopting the ideas of minorities.
ANONYMOUS

Mountains do move...one stone at a time.
RICK BENETEAU

Change should be a friend. It should happen by plan, not by accident.
PHILIP CROSBY

A better world shall emerge based on faith and understanding.
GENERAL DOUGLAS MACARTHUR

Differences

The real death of America will come when everyone is alike.
JAMES T. ELLISON

We all live with the objective of being happy; our lives are all different and yet the same.
ANNE FRANK

How man evolved with such an incredible reservoir of talent and such fantastic diversity isn't completely understood; he knows so little and has nothing to measure himself against.
EDWARD T. HALL

Honest difference of views and honest debate are not disunity. They are the vital process of policy among free men.
HERBERT CLARK HOOVER

Quotable Quotes **Continued**

If we cannot end now our differences, at least we can help make the world safe for diversity.

JOHN F. KENNEDY

Ultimately, America's answer to the intolerant man is diversity, the very diversity which our heritage of religious freedom has inspired.

ROBERT F. KENNEDY

The price of the democratic way of life is a growing appreciation of people's differences, not merely as tolerable, but as the essence of a rich and rewarding human experience.

JEROME NATHANSON

One day our descendants will think it incredible that we paid so much attention to things like the amount of melanin in our skin or the shape of our eyes or our gender instead of the unique identities of each of us as complex human beings.

FRANKLIN THOMAS

Sticks, Stones, and Other Thoughts

A new vision of development is emerging. Development is becoming a people-centered process, whose ultimate goal must be the improvement of the human condition.

BOUTROS BOUTROS-GHALI

A pessimist sees the difficulty in every opportunity; an optimist sees the opportunity in every difficulty.

SIR WINSTON CHURCHILL

Become a fixer, not just a fixture.

ANTHONY J. D'ANGELO

Don't be afraid to take a big step if one is indicated; you can't cross a chasm in two small jumps.

DAVID LLOYD GEORGE

An injustice anywhere is an injustice everywhere.

SAMUEL JOHNSON

Age is opportunity no less than youth itself.

HENRY WADSWORTH LONGFELLOW

Avoid having your ego so close to your position that when your position falls, your ego goes with it.

COLIN POWELL

To divide along the lines of section or caste or creed is un-American.

THEODORE ROOSEVELT

I don't believe in quotas. America was founded on a philosophy of individual rights, not group rights.

CLARENCE THOMAS

Always do right. This will gratify some people and astonish the rest.

MARK TWAIN

A broken bone can heal, but the wound a word opens can fester forever.

JESSAMYN WEST

Helpful Web Sites

Some of the best diversity resources are found on the Internet. Here is a list of Web sites that you might find helpful. This list is meant to be a sample of available information, not an exhaustive reference.

The American Society for Training and Development
http://www.astd.org

Black Engineer.com, the Black Community's Technology News and Information
http://www.blackengineer.com/artman/publish/index.shtml

The Gildeane Group, Inc.
http://www.gildeane.com

Diversity Central—Resources for Cultural Diversity At Work
http://www.diversityhotwire.com

Diversity Inc,
http://shop.diversityinc.com/Merchant2/merchant.mv

Diversity Resources, Inc.
www.diversityresources.com

The Diversity Training Group
http://www.diversitydtg.com

Diversophy.com
http://www.diversophy.com

Education and Professional Diversity Office, Fisher College of Business, The Ohio State University
http://fisher.osu.edu/diversity

Human Rights Campaign
http://www.hrc.org

Intercultural Press
http://interculturalpress.com/shop/index.html

The Institute for Global Communications
http://www.igc.org

HispanicOnline.com
http://www.hispaniconline.com

The Multicultural Advantage
http://www.multiculturaladvantage.com

National Association for Multicultural Education
http://www.nameorg.org

National Forum on People's Differences
http://www.yforum.com

The National Multicultural Institute (NMCI)
http://www.nmci.org

National Women's History Project
http://www.nwhp.org

Office of Diversity Education at Indiana University, Bloomington
http://www.iub.edu/~diversit/diversity/resources.html

The Office of Personnel Management, Federal Government
http://www.leadership.opm.gov/index.cfm

The Public Eye
http://www.publiceye.org/topics.html

Southern Poverty Law Center
http://www.splcenter.org

The Society for Human Resource Management (SHRM)
http://www.shrm.org

University of Maryland Diversity Database
http://www.inform.umd.edu/EdRes/Topic/Diversity

U.S. Latino Web Sites
http://www.public.iastate.edu/~savega/us_latin.htm

Women Entrepreneurship in the 21st Century
http://www.women-21.gov/index2.asp

Workplace Diversity Network of Cornell University
http://www.ilr.cornell.edu/extension/wdn

Templates for Communication

The documents in this section address various aspects of communication related to diversity initiatives and workshops. The templates can be customized to reflect your organization and goals. The templates address the following situations:

- **Compiling Your Organizational Inclusiveness Profile.** This form can be used by the individual(s) charged with beginning a diversity effort within the organization. It will help you gather much of the baseline information needed to establish an appropriate action plan.

- **Training Event Invitation: Generational Awareness.** This invitation is structured to convey a lighthearted, fun message that begins to generate enthusiasm for the upcoming program.

- **Participation Interest Form.** This form can be used when seeking internal volunteers to act as workshop facilitators, brown-bag lunch conveners, or affinity group leaders, or in other roles.

- **Training Reminder Notice (e-mail).** This simple message reminds participants of the date and time scheduled for your session.

- **Event Checklist.** This form helps ensure that all logistics for your session are handled appropriately and helps to avoid any last minute chaos.

- **Common Training Room Setup.** Room setup depends on various factors, including the type and size of the event and special requirements for planned activities. We have found that this room setup is used with the greatest frequency, perhaps because it is typically the best layout to encourage participation.

- **Session Agenda.** This sample agenda illustrates a basic format you can use to provide key stakeholders an easy-to-read overview of your session or event.

- **Welcome Letter.** This letter, signed by senior leaders, (CEO, president, V.P, etc) can be included in participant materials as a way of bringing such key champions "into the room" without them being physically present

- **Facilitator Competencies Evaluation Form.** This form can be used to evaluate yourself or others regarding the core diversity facilitation competencies.

- **Follow-up Letter.** This letter is one example of a follow-up communication that reinforces key concepts covered during the session and reminds participants of their importance.

- **E-mail Follow-up Message.** This brief electronic follow-up message also reinforces specific points with participants.

Templates for Communication Template 1

Compiling Your Organizational Profile

<INSERT COMPANY NAME>

Diversity Initiative: Compiling Our Organizational Profile

<INSERT DATE>

In order to make the highest and best use of our time and resources, we are asking for as much of the following information as possible. If anything is unclear or simply unavailable, please call us directly so we can work out possible alternatives.

1. **Turnover Statistics:** Please provide your turnover data sorted by region and EEO data for the last 2 years.
2. **Exit Interviews:** If you conduct exit interviews, what, if any, trends have you noticed? What are the top three reasons employees leave the organization?
3. **Headcount Targets:** What are your plans over the next 2 years for growth or reduction in the number of personnel? Will some regions be affected more than others?
4. **Hiring Practices:** Please provide an overview of your recruitment, interviewing, and selection process. Policies, training, instructions, and so forth are most helpful.
5. **Career Planning:** Please provide an overview of your career planning systems and employee/management review process. Please provide any relevant forms, processes, training overviews, instructions, and so forth that may help us to better understand your company's procedures.
6. **Competencies:** Please provide any organizational competencies your organization has identified, both for individual contributors and for supervisors, managers, and leaders.
7. **Job Functions:** What are the basic (most common) positions, functions, and roles in your organization? If available, copies of job descriptions are most helpful.
8. **Business Objectives:** What are the organization's top three to five business objectives for this year and next year?
9. **Stakeholders:** Please list the key stakeholders (with job functions and titles) that you see involved with this initiative.
10. **Organizational Structure:** If available, please provide us with your most recent organization charts.
11. **Diversity Council:** Please describe the history to date of the diversity council. How were the members of the council selected? How many? What diversity dimensions are represented in the group? What have been their accomplishments and challenges to date?
12. **Legal Issues:** Have there been any grievances filed or employee lawsuits in the past 2 years? If so, please briefly describe.

Templates for Communication Template 2

Training Event Invitation: Generational Awareness

Note: You can play with creating interesting graphics and color combinations to draw attention to your invitation.

YOU ARE INVITED TO ATTEND A SPECIAL EVENT

Generations in the Workplace: Bridging the Gap

Presented by: *Graciously Hosted by:*

<INSERT SPEAKER NAME/LOGO>   <INSERT HOST NAME/LOGO>

If you are interested in learning more about:
- Why the four generations in today's workforce differ
- How generational differences impact us at work
- What skills will enhance the performance of "intergenerational teams"

Then please join us:

When: <INSERT TIME AND IF FOOD PROVIDED>
Location: <INSERT LOCATION AND DIRECTIONS AS NECESSARY>
Cost: Your time and your active participation

Please R.S.V.P. by (insert date)

Seniors: Please mail a handwritten note
Boomers: Please phone <INSERT CONTACT PERSON> at <PHONE NUMBER>
Gen. Xers: Please e-mail <INSERT NAME> at <E-MAIL ADDRESS>
Gen. Yers: Please IM me TTYL-LOL

...or you can fax your response to <INSERT FAX NUMBER> (It's the big machine in the corner accumulating dust!)...or however you are most comfortable.

Templates for Communication Template 3: Participation Interest Form

Valuing Diversity Facilitator Interest Form

If you are interested in being considered as a facilitator of the

<INSERT COMPANY NAME AND PROGRAM TITLE>

PLEASE COMPLETE AND RETURN BY <INSERT DATE>

If you value wide and differing opinions, know what it feels like to be an outsider and don't want others to feel this way, see the benefit of engaging all employees in your location in the diversity strategy, and are comfortable in front of a group, we would like you to consider helping us take <INSERT COMPANY NAME> to the next level with your co-workers.

If this sounds like an ideal career-development step for you, we will help you learn how to teach the subject matter, articulate the goals of diversity awareness, become more aware of how personal beliefs and values may affect others, and become comfortable facilitating groups and coaching and providing feedback.

If becoming more involved in the diversity strategy through the training process interests you, please fill out the attached form and return it to <INSERT CONTACT NAME, DUE DATE, AND HOW FORM SHOULD BE RETURNED >.

Thanks for your consideration.

Template 3 Participation Interest Form **Continued**

(PLEASE COMPLETE FOLLOWING PAGES):

DEMOGRAPHIC INFORMATION (for use in facilitator selection process only to ensure broadest possible representation and organizational cross section)

1. Name:_____

2. Telephone No.:_____

3. Position (Title):_____

4. Business Unit:_____

5. Location:_____

6. Tenure:_____

7. Gender:_____(Male or Female)

8. Race/Ethnicity:_____

9. Age:_____

10. Sexual Orientation:_____(Heterosexual or GLBT: Gay, Lesbian, Bisexual, or Transgender)

11. Person with Disabilities:_____ (Yes or No)

SELF-ASSESSMENT

12. Please indicate your primary reason(s) for wishing to be considered as a facilitator of the <INSERT PROGRAM TITLE>.

_____

_____

_____

_____

_____

13. What value do you believe you would bring to the training participants if you were selected?

_____

_____

_____

_____

_____

14. What does diversity mean to you?

_____

_____

_____

_____

_____

Template 3 Participation Interest Form Continued

15. Please describe your prior experience(s) with facilitation and training. Please indicate what types of programs (if any) you have delivered.

_____

_____

_____

_____

_____

_____

16. How did you know you were successful in those experiences listed above?

_____

_____

_____

_____

_____

_____

17. What was the most challenging facilitation or training experience you have had? How did you handle it?

_____

_____

_____

_____

_____

_____

18. Are there any restrictions that would prohibit travel or reasons why you could not meet the estimated time commitments, with or without reasonable accommodation?

_____

_____

_____

_____

_____

_____

19. If additional information is needed to complete this process, may we contact you directly? ❏ YES or ❏ NO

THANK YOU!

Templates for Communication **Template 4**

Training Reminder Notice (E-mail)

Subject Line: Training Participation Reminder

We are looking forward to your participation in our <INSERT PROGRAM TITLE>. This reminder notice is simply to confirm with you the date, time, and location of your <INSERT TYPE OF EVENT> with <INSERT NAME OF ORGANIZATION>. Again, you are scheduled for _____

at _____

to be held in the _____.

Please advise us *only* if you are unable to attend by contacting us via return e-mail.

Again, if you have questions, members of the Diversity Council (or appropriate name the organization uses for this group) are readily available.

Templates for Communication Template 5

Event Checklist

General:

- ■ Encourage participation (for those invited) at your locations.
- ■ Register feedback and report back to <INSERT CHAMPION NAME> as needed.
- ■ Answer any participant questions/concerns.

Logistics:

- __ Confirm that conference or training room(s) are blocked.
- __ Provide facilitator with the following by <INSERT DATE>:
  - __ Directions from nearest airport (please indicate) to facility/lodging;
  - __ Preferred lodging nearest to facility—indicate if corporate rates apply;
  - __ Cell phone numbers for contact needs;
  - __ Name and contact information of who facilitator will see upon arrival. Access to building will be needed (<INSERT # OF MINUTES> **minutes** before the event).
- __ Ensure that a flip chart stand, with <INSERT # NEEDED> full pads and working markers will be available for your session (<INSERT # OF WEEKS> week(s) before the event).
- __ Check conference room(s) for cleanliness, chairs, setup, and so forth (<INSERT # OF DAYS> day(s) before the event).
- __ Assist facilitator with any meal needs for the event on (<INSERT DAY/ TIME>).

About the Session—Open Discussion Items:

- ■ Communications: who, when, how?
- ■ Discuss how to handle excused absences.
- ■ Are all on-site locations ideal for this training event? Alternatives?
- ■ Session signage and advance publicity to generate enthusiasm and anticipation?

Templates for Communication **Template 6**

Common Training Room Setup

Suggested Room Setup

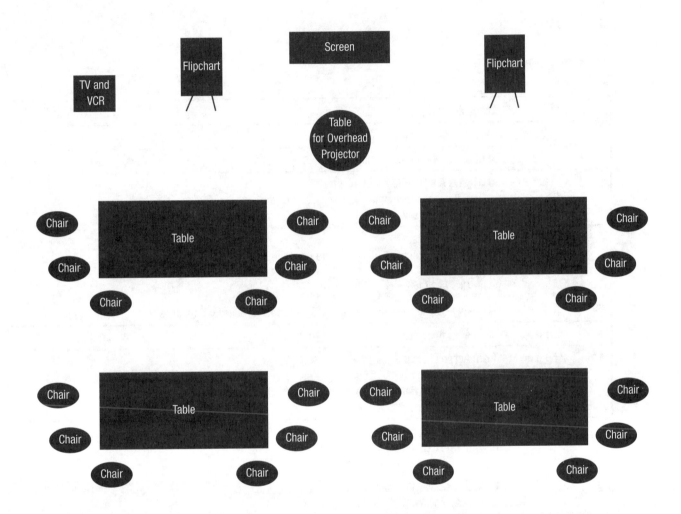

What's Needed in the Room

(<MODIFY THE LIST FOR YOUR SPECIFIC EVENT AND NUMBER OF PARTICIPANTS>)

- 4 tables with 5 or 6 chairs at each table
- Small to medium-size table at front of room for overhead projector
- Overhead projector and screen
- 2 flipcharts and extra pads of flipchart paper
- Markers for the flipcharts
- Masking tape or pins to tape up flipchart paper
- TV with VCR

Templates for Communication Template 7

Session Agenda

<INSERT MEETING OR EVENT TITLE>

<INSERT DATE>

Workshop Outline

	Time	Learning Activity
1.	1:00 p.m.	Kickoff and Positioning
		■ About the Workshop (2 minutes)
		■ Why We Are Here Today (3 minutes) — Reference vision, mission, values, and so forth — State Diversity Team will facilitate future meetings (Use appropriate terminology)
2.	1:05 p.m.	Team Action Plans ■ Celebration of Actions Taken To Date (30 minutes) — Finest Hour — Greatest Challenge ■ Linking Our Regional Actions to Our Organizational Values (60 minutes)
3.	2:35 p.m.	BREAK (15 minutes)
4.	2:50 p.m.	Team Action Plans (continued) ■ Prioritizing Actions (20 minutes) ■ Assignment of Role and Responsibilities (20 minutes) ■ Personal Action Plans (10 minutes)
5.	3:40 p.m.	Closing ■ Wrap Up (10 minutes) — Final Questions and Answers ■ Closing Activity (10 minutes) — "I Appreciate You" Cards
6.	4:00 p.m.	Adjourn

Templates for Communication   Template 8

Welcome Letter

Note: Use the standard communication format for your organization: letterhead, memo format, bulletin, and so forth.

Welcome!

On behalf of <INSERT NAME OF SPONSOR>, I welcome you to the <INSERT WORKSHOP TITLE> workshop.

Interest in this topic has progressed at an exponential rate over the last several decades. As with all the courses in this series, you'll have opportunities to define diversity and examine the components of an inclusive environment. You'll also have opportunities to share things about your culture—things about which you are proud. By learning more about each other and the things you and others believe to be important and unique about your cultures, you can strengthen interpersonal relationships; increase understanding, respect, and valuing; and identify behaviors that create an environment where everyone feels supported and free to do his or her best work.

As businesses and individuals look to the future, they see the need to maximize the effectiveness of every employee—the need to practice and demonstrate inclusion. We created this workshop to better assist those who are charged with meeting the demands of tomorrow, and of today, to succeed with excellence.

With respect,

<INSERT NAME AND TITLE>

Templates for Communication Template 9

Facilitator Competency Assessment

Facilitator: _____   **Date:** _____

To what degree does the facilitator exhibit the following skills/behaviors?

	Exceeds Expectations	Meets Expectations	Does Not Meet Expectations
Diversity Competencies/Program Content			
Shows in-depth conceptual understanding of diversity			
Delivers the program content clearly, accurately, and thoroughly			
Checks that participants are understanding the substance of the material			
Handles the timing, materials, and group activities efficiently			
Links participant comments and experiences to program content			
Continually links program content with stated objectives			
Facilitation Skills			
Pays full attention when participants are speaking			
Uses questioning skills and techniques to successfully solicit ideas and promote participant thinking			
Manages group dynamics by balancing content (the task the group is working on) and process (what is happening between group members)			
Balances facilitator and content expert roles (knowing when it's appropriate to provide content expertise and when to facilitate discussion)			
Oral Presentation			
Works effectively with visuals			
Uses appropriate intonations, voice quality, and pace			
Maintains appropriate eye contact with participants			
Uses appropriate gesturing			
Keeps the audience's attention			
Communication			
Demonstrates sensitivity to others by being aware of needs, feelings, and concerns; reacting appropriately to maintain self-esteem; conveying empathy; and building trust			
Demonstrates oral communication skills through effective listening skills and clear self-expression of knowledge, thoughts, and ideas			

Template 9 Facilitator Competency Assessment **Continued**

	Exceeds Expectations	Meets Expectations	Does Not Meet Expectations
Communication, continued			
Demonstrates effective feedback skills through honesty, listening and responding with empathy, describing specific behavior, and suggesting alternative behavior and opportunities for learning			
Exhibits positive nonverbals such as smiling, acknowledging, and reinforcing			
Co-facilitation			
Interacts respectfully and sensitively with co-facilitator to demonstrate partnership			
Provides support with audiovisuals, tapes, flipcharts, etc.			
Provides a balanced presentation so that both facilitators have equal responsibility in time and content depth			
Gives full attention to the co-facilitator and participants during all activities			
Controlling the Process			
Demonstrates sensitivity to all participants			
Remains neutral and not personally involved in small-group discussions			
Keeps content flow on track and focused on objectives and expected outcomes			
Accepts the reality of the group's level and allows for individual growth			
Handles inappropriate behavior or situations appropriately to maintain a sensitive, trusting, appreciative and respectful learning environment			
Encourages the expression of thoughts, beliefs and feelings and responds in a sensitive, trusting, appreciative and respectful learning environment way			

Template 9 Facilitator Competency Assessment Continued

Facilitator Competency Summary

Content Knowledge	
Strengths	Improvement Opportunities

Group Facilitation Skills	
Strengths	Improvement Opportunities

Templates for Communication **Template 10**

Follow-up Letter

Note: Use the standard communication format for your organization: letterhead, memo format, bulletin, and so forth.

Dear <INSERT PARTICIPANT'S NAME>:

It's been almost a month since we met to review <INSERT PROGRAM TITLE>. We want to thank you again for your great participation and feedback. As often happens in life, we didn't get to "finish" everything we wanted, but we hope that you have taken the time to complete the <INSERT NAME OF POST-SESSION ASSIGNMENT > so that you will be able to reinforce and apply some of the practices we reviewed during our time together. In light of the brief time we spent together, we'd like to follow up by asking you to review some of the following questions.

- <MODIFY THE BULLET POINTS FOR YOUR SPECIFIC EVENT>
- What generations are currently present in your organization?
- How has the "destratification" of generations in your workplace impacted on communication and productivity?
- Like all diverse populations, the mixing of generations in the workplace can lead to an atmosphere of conflict and descent or a foundation for strength and creativity.
- How many of the "Intergenerational Success Keys" do you currently have in place in your organization?

We look forward to seeing you in future programs. Thank you again for your participation and support.

Sincerely,

<INSERT NAME AND TITLE>

The best way to cope with change is to help create it.

L.W. Wynett as it appeared at http://teachers.net/gazette/MAY02/seeds.html.

Templates for Communication Template 11

E-mail Follow-up Message

Dear <INSERT PARTICIPANT'S NAME>,

I wanted to take an opportunity to thank everyone who attended last weeks' meeting—everyone certainly made me feel welcome. Considering the early morning time slot, I was pleasantly surprised by the great discussions, the openness the group showed, and above all the fun that we were able to have. Thank you! You certainly were a great group to speak with about <INSERT PROGRAM TITLE>.

As a reminder of our time together, I have attached a communications overview regarding <INSERT TOPIC> that I hope you find useful.

With Respect,

<INSERT NAME>

Creative Ways to Select "Volunteers"

Selecting participants for activities can be a tricky process. How do you encourage everyone to participate and avoid always using the same eager volunteers? Here are a number of creative ways to choose "volunteers." The person who:

- Has the next or last birthday.

- Has the most number of working televisions in any property (home, vehicles, summer homes, and so forth).

- Woke up earliest today.

- Stayed up latest last night.

- Has the oldest living relative.

- Has the youngest living relative, including pregnancy.

- Gets the 1-2-3 Point! The person at whom the most people are pointing on the count of three is the "volunteer."

- Gets the 1-2-3 Point! Revisited (Use this one only after you've done 1-2-3 Point!) The person at whom the most people are pointing on the count of three gets to pick the "volunteer." Don't tell the participants about the new twist until they've identified a person and think they know who the "volunteer" will be. Lots of fun!

- "The 'volunteer' will be <PAUSE> the last person at your table who stands when I finish speaking."

- Has the longest or shortest hair.

- Has on the most or the least amount of jewelry.

- Has the greatest number of keys with him or her (keys to home, office, car, and so forth).

- Went to the movies most recently. (They'll talk about when and what they saw.)

- Has had the most pets.

- Has the least or most number of siblings.

- Has the most letters in his or her combined first and last names. (Hyphenated last-names are counted.)

- Speaks the most languages.

- Has traveled to the most states within the United States of America.

- Has traveled to the most countries outside of the United States of America.

Contents of the CD-ROM

The CD-ROM that comes with this book includes tools to help you use the activities described in the book and provide you with other support. Specifically, you will find the following items:

- The Activity Matrix from Chapter 1;

- All activities and their accompanying materials;

- Quotable quotes and suggestions for how to use them;

- A list of helpful Web sites;

- Templates for communication; and

- Creative ways to select "volunteers."

Index of Activities & Other Resources

Index

About the Authors

Jonamay Lambert, M.A.

- President and founder of Lambert & Associates, Inc., a Women Business Enterprise firm providing Diversity, Leadership Development and Culture Change solutions.

- Author of the *Diversity Trainers Guides*.

- Board member of the Chicago Council on Urban Affairs.

- Featured speaker at state, national and international conferences.

- Stereotype-breaking experiences: Jonamay is a certified welder and former school principal of a school housed in the Cook County Jail.

Selma Myers, M.A.

- Founder and president Intercultural Development/Myers Consulting.

- Seminars and presentations at major diversity conferences in the United States, Canada, England, Central and South America, and Italy.

- Author of the *Diversity At Work Series of Trainers Guides* as well as *Mediation Across Cultures and Team Building for Diverse Work Groups*.

- Resident lecturer at the Beijing Institute of Technology in China.

- Vice-president and board member, International Visitors Council.

- Fulbright senior consultant, Peru, Argentina and Uruguay, working with bicultural/binational centers offering teacher training programs and management skills for administrators.

For more information about the authors, please view their Web sites:

Jonamay Lambert: **www.lambert-diversity.com**

Selma Myers: **www.myersconsulting.net**

Selected Titles from the
Society for Human Resource Management (SHRM®)

Diverse Teams at Work
By Lee Gardenswartz and Anita Rowe

HR Source Book Series

HIPAA Privacy Source Book
By William S. Hubbartt, SPHR, CCP

Hiring Source Book
By Catherine D. Fyock

Performance Appraisal Source Book
By Mike Deblieux

*Human Resource Essentials: Your Guide to
Starting and Running the HR Function*
By Lin Grensing-Pophal, SPHR

*Manager of Choice: 5 Competencies for
Cultivating Top Talent*
By Nancy S. Ahlrichs

*Managing Employee Retention:
A Strategic Accountability Approach*
By Jack J. Phillips, Ph.D. and
Adele O. Connell, Ph.D.

Practical HR Series

Legal, Effective References: How to Give and Get Them
By Wendy Bliss, J.D., SPHR

*Investigating Workplace Harassment:
How to Be Fair, Thorough, and Legal*
By Amy Oppenheimer, J.D., and
Craig Pratt, MSW, SPHR

Quick! Show Me Your Value
By Theresa Seagraves

*Responsible Restructuring: Creative and
Profitable Alternatives to Layoffs*
By Wayne F. Cascio

Retaining Your Best Employees (In Action Case Studies)
Series Editor Jack J. Phillips

Supervisor's Guide to Labor Relations
By T.O. Collier, Jr.

*Understanding the Federal Wage & Hour Laws:
What Employers Must Know about the
FLSA and its Overtime Regulations*
By Seyfarth Shaw LLP

To Order SHRM Books

SHRM offers a member discount on all books that it publishes or sells.
To order this or any other book published by the Society, contact the SHRMStore®.

ONLINE: www.shrm.org/shrmstore

BY PHONE: (800) 444-5006 (option #1); or (770) 442-8633 (ext. 362);
                or TDD (703) 548-6999

BY FAX: (770) 442-9742

BY MAIL: SHRM Distribution Center
                P.O. Box 930132
                Atlanta, GA 31193-0132
                USA

Selected Titles from the
American Society for Training & Development

Telling Ain't Training
  By Harold D. Stolovitch and Erica J. Keeps

Training Ain't Performance
  By Harold D. Stolovitch and Erica J. Keeps

Quick! Show Me Your Value
  By Theresa Seagraves

Technology for Trainers
  Thomas Toth

ASTD Trainer's WorkShop Series

New Employees Orientation Training
  By Karen Lawson

New Supervisor Training
  John Jones and Chris Chen

Customer Service Training
  Maxine Kamin

Leading Change Training
  Jeffrey and Linda Russell

Leadership Training
  Lou Russell

Coaching Training
  Chris W. Chen

Project Management Training
  Bill Shackelford

Innovation Training
  Ruth Ann Hattori and
  Joyce Wycoff

Sales Training
  Jim Mikula

Communication Training
  Maureen Orey

ASTD Training Basics Series

Trainer Basics
  George M. Piskurich

Presentation Basics
  Robert J. Rosania

Training Design Basics
  Saul Carliner

Facilitation Basics
  Donald V. McCain and
  Deborah Tobey

Performance Basics
  Joe Willmore

To Order ASTD Books

ASTD offers a member discount on all books that it publishes or sells. To order or browse other books published by ASTD Press, contact:

ONLINE: store.astd.org

BY PHONE: (800) 628-2783 or (703) 683-8100 (international)

BY FAX: (703) 683-1523

BY MAIL: ASTD Product Fulfillment
        PO Box 1567
        Merrifield, VA 22116-1567

Using the Accompanying CD ROM

For your convenience, the following materials in the book are on the accompanying CD-ROM:

- The Activity Matrix from Chapter 1;

- All activities and their accompanying materials;

- Quotable quotes and suggestions for how to use them;

- A list of helpful Web sites;

- Templates for communication; and

- Creative ways to select "volunteers."

The materials are usable on a PC computer. Forms are included in two formats: Portable Document Format and Rich Text Format. Purchasers of the book may use the materials on the CD-ROM as part of their own training materials providing that they include the full crediting information that appears on the bottom of each page.

Portable Document Format (PDF) Files

The PDF files contain the materials exactly as they appear in the book—with all formatting. To open the files and print them out, all you need is the free Adobe® Acrobat® Reader, which is included on the CD-ROM. See "Getting Started," below. To customize or modify the PDF materials, you need the full Adobe® Acrobat® system. If you do not have that program on your computer, you can get information and purchase it from **www.acrobat.com**.

Rich Text Format (RTF) Files

The RTF files contain all of the text of the materials but not all of the formatting. RFT files can be opened in many word processing programs and provide an easy-to-modify version of the materials.

Acrobat Reader 5.0.5 System Requirements

The PDF files on this disc are compatible with Acrobat Reader versions 4.0 and higher.

Your computer needs:

- an Intel® Pentium® processor;

- Microsoft® Windows® 95 OSR 2.0, Windows 98 SE, Windows Millennium, Windows NT®;

- 4.0 with Service Pack 5, Windows 2000, or Windows XP;

- 64 MB of RAM;

- 24 MB of available hard-disk space; and

- Additional 70 MB of hard-disk space for Asian fonts (optional).

Getting Started

To access the files on the CD-ROM, insert the CD-ROM into your compact disc drive. The disc will AutoRun and prompt you to install Acrobat Reader 5.0.5, if required, or open the Main Menu. Follow the directions on your screen.

STOP!

Please read the following before opening the CD-ROM accompanying this book.

This software contains files to help you use the materials described in the accompanying book. By opening the CD-ROM package, you are agreeing to be bound by the following agreement:

Once you open the seal on the software package, this book and the CD ROM are nonrefundable. (With the seal unbroken, the book and CD-ROM are refundable only under the terms generally allowed by the seller.)

This software product is protected by copyright and all rights are reserved by the Society for Human Resource Management (SHRM®) and its licensors. Purchasers of the book may use the materials on the CD-ROM as part of their own training materials providing that they include the full crediting information that appears on the bottom of each page. You are licensed to use this software on a single computer. Copying the software to another medium or format for use on a single computer is permitted and therefore does not violate the U.S. Copyright Law. Copying the software for any other purposes is not permitted and is therefore a violation of the U.S. Copyright Law.

This software product is sold as is without warranty of any kind, either express or implied, including but not limited to the implied warranty of merchantability and fitness for a particular purpose. Neither SHRM nor its dealers or distributors assumes any liability for any alleged or actual damages arising from the use of or the inability to use this software. (Some states do not allow the exclusion of implied warranties, so the exclusion may not apply to you if you receive this product in such a state.)